BARRON'S
FOREIGN LANGUAGE GUIDES

W9-CCB-349

JAPANESE
Grammar

THIRD EDITION

Nobuo Akiyama
Adjunct Professor, Japanese Language
The Paul H. Nitze School of Advanced International Studies
The Johns Hopkins University

Carol Akiyama
Language Training Consultant
Washington, D.C.

BARRON'S

All inquiries should be addressed to:
Barron's Educational Series, Inc.
250 Wireless Boulevard
Hauppauge, New York 11788
www.barronseduc.com

ISBN-13: 978-0-7641-4774-6
Library of Congress Control Number 2011934993

PRINTED IN CHINA
9 8 7 6 5 4 3 2 1

Contents

Preface

This book is designed for students, businesspeople, and others who want to improve their knowledge of Japanese grammar. It enables you to reflect on what you already know, to reinforce your skills, and to fill in the gaps.

Whether you are just beginning your study of Japanese or have some basic Japanese and want to refresh your memory, this book is for you. Previous knowledge has not been taken for granted; definitions and explanations are simple and concise, and examples use and reuse a core of basic vocabulary.

The book is divided into three sections:

- In the Basics section you will find a nontechnical and easy-to-follow discussion of Japanese sounds, spelling conventions, and word-order patterns.
- In the Parts of Speech section you will find the nouns, pronouns, particles, verbs, adjectives, and adverbs that make up the Japanese language.
- In the Special Topics section you will find numbers, expressions for telling time, useful words and phrases, borrowed words, synonyms, antonyms, and more.

Our Japanese–English Vocabulary section shows all the Japanese words in the book along with their English meaning. Color is used to highlight important points of grammar or vocabulary, and the "Tip" boxes help you understand Japanese language and culture.

We would like to thank the following people for their invaluable help with this project: Masako Nanto, School of Language Studies, Foreign Service Institute, Department of State; Diane Roth, Editor, and Dimitry Popow, Languages Editor, Barron's Educational Series, Inc.

And many thanks to the teachers and students of Japanese who have shared with us their welcome, helpful, and supportive comments about the previous editions of this book.

Nobuo and Carol Akiyama

How to Use This Book

In the chapters that follow, a numerical decimal system has been used with the symbol § in front of it. This was done so that you may find quickly and easily the reference to a particular point in basic Japanese grammar when you use the index. For example, if you look up the entry "particles" in the index, you will find the reference given as §6. Sometimes additional § reference numbers are given when the entry you consulted is mentioned in other areas in the chapter §.

The Basics

§1.

Pronunciation Guide

§1.1   WHAT ARE VOWELS AND CONSONANTS?

There are two kinds of sounds in any language.

- *Vowels* are produced by air passing out through the mouth without being blocked. The letters that represent these sounds are **a, e, i, o, u**.
- *Consonants*, on the other hand, are produced by blockage (partial or complete) of the air. The remaining alphabet letters are used to represent consonant sounds: **b, c, d**, etc.

Japanese isn't difficult to pronounce if you follow a few simple guidelines. Take the time to read this section, and try out each sound presented.

§1.2   VOWELS

Tip	If you have studied Spanish, it may help you to know that Japanese vowels are more like those of Spanish than English.

The following vowels are short and pure, with *no glide*—that is, they are not diphthongs.

1

JAPANESE VOWEL	ENGLISH EQUIVALENT	EXAMPLE
a	as in f**a**ther	**a**kai (*ah-kah-ee*) red
e	as in m**e**n	**e**bi (*eh-bee*) shrimp
i	as in s**ee**	**i**mi (*ee-mee*) meaning
o	as in b**oa**t	**o**toko (*oh-toh-koh*) male
u	as in f**oo**d	**u**ma (*oo-mah*) horse

The following vowels are like the ones above, but lengthened.

JAPANESE VOWEL	ENGLISH EQUIVALENT	EXAMPLE
ā	as in f**a**ther, but lengthened	bat**ā** (*bah-tah̄*) butter
ei	as in m**e**n, but lengthened	**ei**go (*eh̄-goh*) English
ii	as in s**ee**, but lengthened	**ii**haru (*ēe-hah-roo*) insist
ō	as in b**oa**t, but lengthened	**ō**sama (*oh̄-sah-mah*) king
ū	as in f**oo**d, but lengthened	y**ū**bin (*yōo-been*) mail

Macrons

A *macron*, or bar, above a vowel means it should be lengthened.

Example

butter / batā / *bah-tāh*

In the above word, the macron above the second vowel means you should hold the sound twice as long as you normally would.

And keep in mind these points:

- Long vowels are important. Pronouncing a long vowel incorrectly can result in a different word or even an unintelligible one.

  For example,   obasan (*oh-bah-sahn*) means **aunt**
  obāsan (*oh-bāh-sahn*) means **grandmother**

  ojisan (*oh-jee-sahn*) means **uncle**
  ojiisan (*oh-jēē-sahn*) means **grandfather**

  seki (*seh-kee*) means **seat**
  seiki (*sēh-kee*) means **century**

  (For more examples, see §19.)

- Sometimes the **i** and the **u** aren't pronounced. This usually occurs between voiceless consonants (**p**, **t**, **k**, **ch**, **f**, **h**, **s**, **sh**), or at the end of a word following a voiceless consonant.

  ### Examples

  sukiyaki   (*skee-yah-kee*)

This word for a popular Japanese dish begins with **skee**, not **soo**. The **u** is not pronounced.

  tabemashita (*tah-beh-mahsh-tah*) **I ate**

The **i** is not pronounced.

§1.3 CONSONANTS

With a few exceptions, Japanese consonants are similar to those of English. Note those that are different:

f	The English **f** is pronounced with a passage of air between the upper teeth and the lower lip. To make the Japanese **f**, blow air lightly between your lips as if you were just beginning a whistle.
g	Always as in **g**o, never as in a**g**e. You may also hear it pronounced as the **ng** sound in si**ng** but not at the beginning of a word.
r	This is different from the English **r**. To make the Japanese **r**, lightly touch the tip of your tongue to the bony ridge behind the upper teeth, almost in the English **d** position. It's more like the Spanish **r**, but it's not trilled.
s	Always hissed, as in **s**o, never voiced, as in hi**s** or or plea**s**ure.

And note the following points as well:

- If you have trouble making a consonant the Japanese way, your English pronunciation will still be intelligible.
- Some Japanese consonants are doubled. In English, this is just a feature of spelling and often doesn't affect pronunciation. In Japanese, the doubling is important and may change the meaning of a word.

Example

Kite kudasai (*kee-teh koo-dah-sah-ee*) means
"Please put it (clothing) on."

Kitte kudasai (*Keet-teh koo-dah-sah-ee*) means
"Please cut it."

(For more examples, see **§20**.)

Tip

> In a word with a doubled consonant, don't say the
> consonant twice—simply hold the sound longer.

§2.

The Japanese Writing System

§2.2 DIRECTION AND CHARACTERS

Traditionally, Japanese is written from top to bottom and from right to left. But it is also written horizontally and from left to right, as in English.

Japanese writing uses three kinds of characters:

kanji (*kahn-jee*)	漢字
hiragana (*hee-rah-gah-nah*)	ひらがな
katakana (*kah-tah-kah-nah*)	カタカナ

Hiragana and katakana are also called **kana** (*kah-nah*). All three are used together in Japanese writing.

§2.2 KANJI

Chinese and Japanese are completely different languages. But beginning in the fourth or fifth century, Japanese adopted written symbols and many vocabulary items from Chinese. In Japan, these symbols or Chinese characters are called **kanji**. They represent both meaning and sound, and often one kanji has more than one pronunciation (or reading, as it's commonly called) and meaning.

Japanese people learn about 2,000 kanji by the end of junior high school. Those are the basic characters used in newspapers, magazines, and school textbooks. Most Japanese know several thousand additional kanji as well.

Kanji range from simple, with one or two strokes, to complex, with many strokes needed to make one character. Some look like pictures, or line drawings, of the words they represent.

Examples

mountain	yama (*yah-mah*)	山
river	kawa (*kah-wah*)	川

These two together form Yamakawa, 山川 a family name. Here are some more kanji:

Japan	Nihon (*nee-hon*)	日本
person	hito (*hee-toh*)	人
	jin (*jeen*)	
Japanese	Nihonjin (*nee-hon-jeen*)	日本人

§2.3 HIRAGANA AND KATAKANA

Hiragana and **Katakana** symbols represent the sounds of syllables. Hiragana is used for native Japanese words and grammatical elements, and katakana is mainly for words of foreign origin. Each is a kind of alphabet, or syllabary, of 46 basic characters or sounds.

The following example will show you how the elements are used together.

Sumisu san, Nihon e yōkoso. / **Welcome to Japan**, **Mr. Smith**. スミスさん、日本へようこそ。

Smith	**Mr.**	**Japan**	**to welcome**	
|	|	|	|	|
Sumisu	san	Nihon	e	yōkoso
スミス	さん	日本	へ	ようこそ
katakana	hiragana	kanji	hiragana	

The **hiragana** and **katakana** charts provided here will be useful if you continue your study of Japanese.

HIRAGANA				
あ **a** (ah)	い **i** (ee)	う **u** (oo)	え **e** (eh)	お **o** (oh)
か **ka** (kah)	き **ki** (kee)	く **ku** (koo)	け **ke** (keh)	こ **ko** (koh)
さ **sa** (sah)	し **shi** (shee)	す **su** (soo)	せ **se** (seh)	そ **so** (soh)
た **ta** (tah)	ち **chi** (chee)	つ **tsu** (tsoo)	て **te** (teh)	と **to** (toh)
な **na** (nah)	に **ni** (nee)	ぬ **nu** (noo)	ね **ne** (neh)	の **no** (noh)
は **ha** (hah)	ひ **hi** (hee)	ふ **fu** (foo)	へ **he** (heh)	ほ **ho** (hoh)
ま **ma** (mah)	み **mi** (mee)	む **mu** (moo)	め **me** (meh)	も **mo** (moh)
や **ya** (yah)		ゆ **yu** (yoo)		よ **yo** (yoh)
ら **ra** (rah)	り **ri** (ree)	る **ru** (roo)	れ **re** (reh)	ろ **ro** (roh)
わ **wa** (wah)				を **o** (oh)
ん **n**				
が **ga** (gah)	ぎ **gi** (gee)	ぐ **gu** (goo)	げ **ge** (geh)	ご **go** (goh)
ざ **za** (zah)	じ **ji** (jee)	ず **zu** (zoo)	ぜ **ze** (zeh)	ぞ **zo** (zoh)
だ **da** (dah)	ぢ **ji** (jee)	づ **zu** (zoo)	で **de** (deh)	ど **do** (doh)
ば **ba** (bah)	び **bi** (bee)	ぶ **bu** (boo)	べ **be** (beh)	ぼ **bo** (boh)
ぱ **pa** (pah)	ぴ **pi** (pee)	ぶ **pu** (poo)	ぺ **pe** (peh)	ぽ **po** (poh)
きゃ **kya** (kyah)		きゅ **kyu** (kyoo)		きょ **kyo** (kyoh)
しゃ **sha** (shah)		しゅ **shu** (shoo)		しょ **sho** (shoh)
ちゃ **cha** (chah)		ちゅ **chu** (choo)		ちょ **cho** (choh)
にゃ **nya** (nyah)		にゅ **nyu** (nyoo)		にょ **nyo** (nyoh)
ひゃ **hya** (hyah)		ひゅ **hyu** (hyoo)		ひょ **hyo** (hyoh)
みゃ **mya** (myah)		みゅ **myu** (myoo)		みょ **myo** (myoh)
りゃ **rya** (ryah)		りゅ **ryu** (ryoo)		りょ **ryo** (ryoh)
ぎゃ **gya** (gyah)		ぎゅ **gyu** (gyoo)		ぎょ **gyo** (gyoh)
じゃ **ja** (jah)		じゅ **ju** (joo)		じょ **jo** (joh)
びゃ **bya** (byah)		びゅ **byu** (byoo)		びょ **byo** (byoh)
ぴゃ **pya** (pyah)		ぴゅ **pyu** (pyoo)		ぴょ **pyo** (pyoh)

KATAKANA

ア a (ah)	イ i (ee)	ウ u (oo)	エ e (eh)	オ o (oh)
カ ka (kah)	キ ki (kee)	ク ku (koo)	ケ ke (keh)	コ ko (koh)
サ sa (sah)	シ shi (shee)	ス su (soo)	セ se (seh)	ソ so (soh)
タ ta (tah)	チ chi (chee)	ツ tsu (tsoo)	テ te (teh)	ト to (toh)
ナ na (nah)	ニ ni (nee)	ヌ nu (noo)	ネ ne (neh)	ノ no (noh)
ハ ha (hah)	ヒ hi (hee)	フ fu (foo)	ヘ he (heh)	ホ ho (hoh)
マ ma (mah)	ミ mi (mee)	ム mu (moo)	メ me (meh)	モ mo (moh)
ヤ ya (yah)		ユ yu (yoo)		ヨ yo (yoh)
ラ ra (rah)	リ ri (ree)	ル ru (roo)	レ re (reh)	ロ ro (roh)
ワ wa (wah)			ヲ o (oh)	

ン n				

ガ ga (gah)	ギ gi (gee)	グ gu (goo)	ゲ ge (geh)	ゴ go (goh)
ザ za (zah)	ジ ji (jee)	ズ zu (zoo)	ゼ ze (zeh)	ゾ zo (zoh)
ダ da (dah)	ヂ ji (jee)	ヅ zu (zoo)	デ de (deh)	ド do (doh)
バ ba (bah)	ビ bi (bee)	ブ bu (boo)	ベ be (beh)	ボ bo (boh)

パ pa (pah)	ピ pi (pee)	プ pu (poo)	ペ pe (peh)	ポ po (poh)
ファ fa (fah)	フィ fi (fee)	フ fu (foo)	フェ fe (feh)	フォ fo (foh)

キャ kya (kyah)		キュ kyu (kyoo)		キョ kyo (kyoh)
シャ sha (shah)		シュ shu (shoo)		ショ sho (shoh)
チャ cha (chah)		チュ chu (choo)		チョ cho (choh)
ニャ nya (nyah)		ニュ nyu (nyoo)		ニョ nyo (nyoh)
ヒャ hya (hyah)		ヒュ hyu (hyoo)		ヒョ hyo (hyoh)
ミャ mya (myah)		ミュ myu (myoo)		ミョ myo (myoh)
リャ rya (ryah)		リュ ryu (ryoo)		リョ ryo (ryoh)

ギャ gya (gyah)		ギュ gyu (gyoo)		ギョ gyo (gyoh)
ジャ ja (jah)		ジュ ju (joo)		ジョ jo (joh)
ビャ bya (byah)		ビュ byu (byoo)		ビョ byo (byoh)
ピャ pya (pyah)		ピュ pyu (pyoo)		ピョ pyo (pyoh)

§2.4 ROMAJI

The commonly used expression for the romanization of Japanese words is **romaji**. Although there are several systems of romaji, the most widely used, and the one used in this book, is a modified version of the Hepburn system.

§3.

Word Order

§3.1 WHAT IS A SENTENCE?

A *sentence* is an organized series of words which enables us to make a statement, ask a question, express a thought, offer an opinion, and so forth. In writing, an English sentence starts with a capital letter and ends with a period, a question mark, or an exclamation mark. In writing (using romaji), a Japanese sentence starts with a capital letter, and ends with a period, not a question mark or an exclamation mark.

Examples

Yoko is Japanese. / Yōko san wa Nihonjin desu. (statement)

Is Yoko Japanese? / Yōko san wa Nihonjin desu ka. (question)

Yoko, be careful! / Yōko san ki o tsukete kudasai. (exclamation)

§3.2 THE ENGLISH SENTENCE

English is a *Subject-Verb-Object* language. (So are French, German, Spanish, and Italian.) This means that in a typical sentence (a statement, not a question), the subject comes first, the verb next, and the object last. This kind of word order sequence for the sentence is sometimes referred to by the initials **SVO** (an SVO language).

Examples

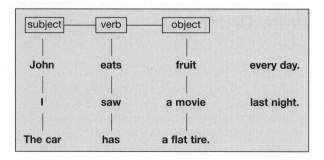

Understanding this principle of word order is important because, as we shall see in **§3.3**, the word order in Japanese is different.

English sentences have two basic parts, a *subject* and a *predicate*.

- The subject is "who" or "what" the sentence is about. A subject must contain a noun or pronoun. In a statement, the subject is usually the first element in the sentence.

Examples

- The predicate is that part of the sentence that expresses what is said about the subject. It usually can be found directly after the subject, it must include a verb, and it includes everything remaining in the sentence that is not part of the subject.

Examples

§3.3 THE JAPANESE SENTENCE

§3.3–1 Subject-Object-Verb Sentences

Japanese is a *Subject-Object-Verb* language. (So are Korean, Mongolian, and Turkish.) Thus, in a typical sentence, the subject comes first, the object next, and the verb last. This kind of word order sequence for the sentence is sometimes referred to by the initials **SOV** (an SOV language).

Examples

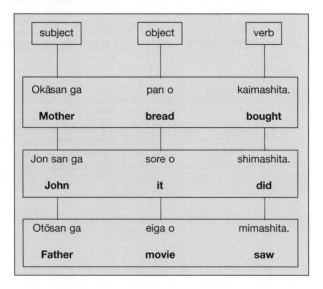

subject	object	verb
Okāsan ga	pan o	kaimashita.
Mother	**bread**	**bought**
Jon san ga	sore o	shimashita.
John	**it**	**did**
Otōsan ga	eiga o	mimashita.
Father	**movie**	**saw**

The significant difference from English here is that the verb must come at the *end* of the sentence.

- What about questions? The word order remains the same. But remember: Japanese does not use question marks. A sentence becomes a question by adding the particle *ka* at the end. You can think of *ka* as a question mark. (Particles, an important Part of Speech in Japanese, will be discussed in **§6**.)

Examples

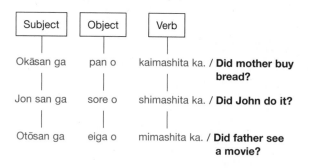

Subject	Object	Verb
Okāsan ga	pan o	kaimashita ka. / **Did mother buy bread?**
Jon san ga	sore o	shimashita ka. / **Did John do it?**
Otōsan ga	eiga o	mimashita ka. / **Did father see a movie?**

§3.3–2 Subject and Predicate

Tip

Japanese sentences *may* have a subject or a topic, but they *must* have a predicate. (The subject is followed by the particle *ga*, and the topic by the particle *wa*. See **§6**.)

- The *predicate* is the core of the Japanese sentence. It comes at the end, and it must be a verb or a verbal form. In Japanese, a verbal form may be a noun plus copula (like English **is** or **are**. See **§7.6**), or a verbal adjective.

Examples

- In addition to the *subject* or topic, there may, of course, be other elements in the sentence—*object*, *indirect object*, *adverb*, and so forth. They come before the predicate, and are not considered part of it.
- Two principles hold true for word order in a Japanese sentence:

  The predicate must come at the end of the sentence.

  A particle must immediately follow the word or words it marks.

- Other than this, word order is not rigid. The subject or topic usually comes first, although an adverb of time may precede it or follow it. Expressions of time usually precede expressions of place. Most modifiers precede the words they modify.

Examples

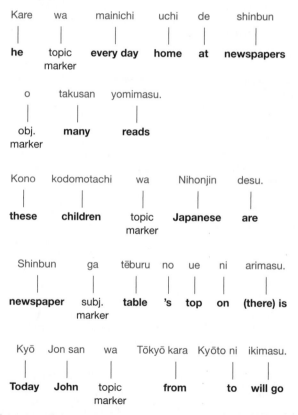

Kare	wa	mainichi	uchi	de	shinbun
he	topic marker	**every day**	**home**	**at**	**newspapers**

o	takusan	yomimasu.
obj. marker	**many**	**reads**

Kono	kodomotachi	wa	Nihonjin	desu.
these	**children**	topic marker	**Japanese**	**are**

Shinbun	ga	tēburu	no	ue	ni	arimasu.
newspaper	subj. marker	**table**	**'s**	**top**	**on**	**(there) is**

Kyō	Jon san	wa	Tōkyō kara	Kyōto ni	ikimasu.
Today	**John**	topic marker	**from**	**to**	**will go**

Kanojo wa honya de hon o kaimashita.

| she | topic marker | bookstore | at | book | obj. marker | bought |

- With a question, the word order is the same. As you now know, the particle *ka* at the end of the sentence makes a statement into a question.

Example

Kanojo wa honya de hon o kaimashita ka. / **Did she buy a book at the bookstore?**

she topic marker

- If a question uses a question word (*when*, *who*, *what*, etc.), it normally comes after the subject or topic, but this is not rigid.

Examples

Kanojo wa itsu honya de hon o kaimashita ka. / **When did she buy a book at the bookstore?**

she topic marker when

Kanojo wa naze honya de hon o kaimashita ka. / **Why did she buy a book at the bookstore?**

she topic marker why

Dare ga honya de hon o kaimashita ka. / **Who bought a book at the bookstore?**

who subj. marker

Sore	wa	donna hon desu ka. / **What kind of**
		book is it?
it	topic	what kind of
	marker	

§3.3–3 Incomplete Sentences

In most languages, words that can be understood or implied
from the context of the situation can be left out of a sentence.
In Japanese, it is the subject or topic that is omitted, not the
predicate. If the situation is clear without the subject or topic,
Japanese tend to leave it out.

Example

Kore wa nan desu ka. / **What is this?**
  Kore wa hon desu. / **This is a book.**
  or
  Hon desu.

  book is

   In English, this question could be answered with just the
noun: **A book**.
   In Japanese, the copula, or verb **to be** is needed too.
Remember, a Japanese sentence must have a predicate, or
verb form. Look at some more examples.

Example

Anata wa   nani o   kaimashita ka. / **What did you buy?**

   you   what   did buy

Tip

> Although this sentence is gramatically correct, the
> Japanese prefer to omit the **you** which would be
> obvious from the context.

Example

Nani o kaimashita ka. / **What did (you) buy?**

Hon o kaimashita. / **(I) bought a book.**

In a sense, these shouldn't be called "incomplete sentences" because, to the Japanese, they are quite complete!

Parts of Speech

§4.

Nouns

§4.1 WHAT ARE NOUNS?

A *noun* is a word that names or refers to a person, a place, or a thing. A thing may be a quality or a concept.

There are two main types of nouns:

- A *proper* noun names a particular person, place, or thing. In English, all proper nouns are capitalized. The Japanese concept of proper nouns is more limited. In romaji (see §**2.4**), names of persons or places, for example, are capitalized, but days of the week and months of the year are not. The words for other languages are capitalized, but not the word for English: *eigo*.

  Examples

  Jon san wa, Tōkyō ni ikimasu. / **John is going to Tokyo.**

21

noun	noun	noun
Jon	getsuyōbi	Tōkyō
	Monday	

Jon san wa, getsuyōbi ni Tōkyō ni ikimasu. / **John is going to Tokyo on Monday.**

nouns		nouns	
kayōbi	/ **Tuesday**	sangatsu	/ **March**
kinyōbi	/ **Friday**	rokugatsu	/ **June**

nouns	
Furansugo	/ **French** (language)
Chūgokugo	/ **Chinese** (language)
eigo	/ **English** (language)

- A *common* noun does not name a particular person, place, or thing.

    Examples

    hon / **book**   otokonoko / **boy**   onnanoko / **girl**

§4.2 GENDER

Japanese nouns do not have *gender*. There are no special endings to show masculine, feminine, or neuter forms.

§4.3 ARTICLES

Japanese does not use *articles* before nouns. There are no words to correspond to English **a**, **an**, or **the**.

§4.4 NUMBER

Number means that a word can be *singular* (referring to one person, thing, etc.) or *plural* (referring to more than one). With most Japanese nouns, number is not an issue. *The same word is used for one or for more than one.*

Examples

hon / **book, books**

shinbun / **newspaper, newspapers**

kuruma / **car, cars**

uchi / **house, houses**

ki / **tree, trees**

te / **hand, hands**

Hon o motte imasu. / **I have a book.**

Hon o motte imasu. / **I have some books.**

- For nouns referring to people, the plural suffix -*tachi* may be used, although it isn't required.

Examples

kodomo / **child, children**

otokonoko / **boy, boys**

onnanoko / **girl, girls**

hahaoya / **mother, mothers**

sensei / **teacher, teachers**

kodomotachi / **children**

otokonokotachi / **boys**

onnanokotachi / **girls**

hahaoyatachi / **mothers**

senseitachi / **teachers**

- When -*tachi* is used with someone's name, it usually refers to the person and his or her family or group.

Examples

Tanaka san tachi / **Mr. Tanaka and his family**

Tomoko san tachi / **Tomoko and her group**

§4.5 NAMES

Japanese use *family names first*, and *first names last*.

Examples

When Japanese introduce themselves to each other, they say the family name first. However, they know that English speakers do it the opposite way.

Tip	Japanese prefer family names, not first names. Japanese adults rarely use first names. Even among friends, family names are the rule, first names the exception. Unless a Japanese specifically asks you to use his or her first name, you should use the family name.

With children, it's different. Japanese use young children's first names followed by the title *chan*, older children's first names followed by *san* (see **§4.6**).

Sometimes *kun* is used for boys instead of *chan*. The switch from *chan* to *san* or *kun* occurs around 12 years of age.

§4.6 TITLES

The Japanese word that corresponds to English **Mr.**, **Mrs.**, **Miss**, and **Ms.** is *san*. The Japanese always use *san* (or other, more formal titles of respect) with proper names. Even among family members or close personal friends who use first names with each other, *san* follows the name.

Tip	Be sure to use *san* in direct address (when speaking directly to someone), and when referring to someone else. *Never* use *san* to refer to yourself.

Examples

Tanaka san, kōhī wa ikaga desu ka. / **Mr. Tanaka, would you like some coffee?**

Merī san wa, kyō gakkō ni imasu ka. / **Is Mary at school today?**

But note the following:

Watakushi wa, John Smith desu. / **I'm John Smith.**

§4.7 POLITENESS

The prefix *o-* before certain nouns expresses *politeness*. (This is also used with verbs and adjectives. See **§7** and **§8**.)

Examples

namae, onamae / **name**   kane, okane / **money**

sake, osake / **rice wine**   furo, ofuro / **bath**

hashi, ohashi / **chopsticks**   tegami, otegami / **letter**

A variation of this form is *go-*, which is used with words of Chinese origin.

hon, gohon / **book**   kekkon, gokekkon / **marriage**

Note the following about the prefixes *o-* and *go-*:

- Although both men and women may use the above forms, in some cases, these prefixes would be used only by women, as in the "o" forms in examples below.

  Examples

  niku, oniku / **meat**   yasai, oyasai / **vegetables**

- Some words are *always* used with the polite prefix. The *o-* and *go-* are now part of the words:

  Examples

  ocha / **Japanese tea**   gohan / **cooked rice, meal**

| Tip | • These prefixes cannot be used with all nouns. It's best to use them only when you are certain they are correct, as with the examples above. |

§4.8 COMPOUND NOUNS

When two nouns are used together to make a *compound noun*, they are usually joined by the particle *no*.

  Examples

  rekishi no kurasu / **history class**

  eigo no sensei / **English teacher**

  apāto no biru / **apartment building**

Some compound nouns may be formed *without* the *no*, however.

Examples

kōhī jawan / **coffee cup**

kankō basu / **tour bus**

bōeki gaisha / **trading company**

§4.9 NOUN SUFFIXES

- The suffix *-ya*, when added to a noun, means the place or shop where that thing is sold, or the person or shopkeeper who sells it.

    Examples

    niku / **meat** ──────────→ nikuya / **butcher shop, butcher**

    hon / **book** ──────────→ honya / **bookstore, clerk, owner**

    kamera / **camera** ────→ kameraya / **camera shop, clerk, owner**

- When referring to the clerk or shopkeeper, the title *san* is used:

    Examples

    nikuya san / **butcher**

    kameraya san / **camera shop clerk**

- The suffix *-ka*, when added to a noun, means a person with expertise or special knowledge on that subject.

Examples

seiji / **politics** ──────────→ seijika / **politician**

hyōron / **commentary** ────────→ hyōronka / **critic, commentator**

shōsetsu / **novel** ──────────→ shōsetsuka / **novelist**

geijutsu / **art** ──────────→ geijutsuka / **artist**

§5.

Pronouns

§5.1 WHAT ARE PRONOUNS?

A *pronoun* is a word that takes the place of a noun. Here are some common English pronouns: **I, you, he, she, it, we, they**. These are personal pronouns used as *subjects*. Other common English pronouns are **me, him, her, us, them**. These are personal pronouns used as *objects*. **You** and **it**, of course, may be subjects or objects. In addition to these, there are other kinds of pronouns, such as *possessive* (**mine, yours, his**, etc.), *demonstrative* (**this, that**), and *interrogative* (**who, where, what**, etc.)

Japanese pronoun usage is quite different from that of English, as you will see from the following discussion.

§5.2 PERSONAL PRONOUNS

Personal pronouns in Japanese refer to people, not things or ideas. Japanese has no equivalent to the English **it** in this category.

Tip

- When the meaning can be understood from the context, the Japanese prefer *not* to use personal pronouns. Use these with care, and be sure to read the information that follows.

29

Singular	Plural
watakushi / **I, me**	watakushitachi / **we, us**
anata / **you**	anatatachi / **you** anatagata / **you** (polite)
kare / **he, him**	karera / **they, them** (all male or male and female)
kanojo / **she, her**	kanojotachi / **they, them** (female) kanojora / **they, them** (female)

Tip	Informal usage watashi / **I, me** atashi / **I, me** (female)

§5.2–1 Special Usage

anata / **you**

- Avoid using this whenever possible. When speaking to someone directly, try to use the person's name and *san* instead.

Example

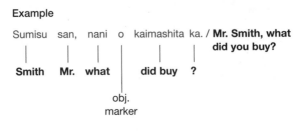

Sumisu san, nani o kaimashita ka. / **Mr. Smith, what did you buy?**

Smith   Mr.   what   did buy   ?

obj.
marker

- When speaking to a teacher, a doctor, a dentist, or a member of the Diet (the Japanese legislature), use the word *sensei*, either alone, or after the person's last name. *Sensei*, which literally means "teacher," may also be used with others not listed above. A teacher can be one who has achieved success or earned respect in his or her field. You can use *sensei*, for example, to address an artist, writer, architect, musician, or other talented person.

Example

Sensei, ogenki desu ka. / **Sir (teacher), how have you been?**

If you are speaking to a group, you can use the following expressions for "you" (plural):

Example

mina san / **everyone (you all)**   mina sama / **everyone (you all)**

| mina / **everyone** | + | san |

or

| sama | (very polite, and more formal than *san*) |

Examples

Mina san, ohayō gozaimasu. / **Good morning, everyone.**

Mina sama, sayōnara. / **Goodbye, everyone!**

kare / **he**   kanojo / **she**

* Whenever possible, when referring to a third person, use the person's name.

Example

Sumisu san wa Nyūyōku kara kimashita ka. / **Is Mrs. Smith from New York?**

This is better than saying, "Is *she* from New York?" Of course, if it is clear who the subject is, it can be left out entirely.

* Several other terms can be used instead of the pronouns *kare*, *kanojo*, and their plural forms. The Japanese prefer these:

Singular	Plural
ano hito / **that person**	ano hitotachi / **those persons**
ano kata / **that person (polite)**	ano katagata / **those persons (polite)**

Examples

Kinō |ano hito| ni aimashita ka. / **Did you see him (that person) yesterday?**

that person

|Ano katagata| wa kinō irasshaimashita. / **They (those persons) were here yesterday.**

those persons

§5.2–2   Case

Case refers to the form of a pronoun which shows its relationship to other words in a sentence.

In English, the personal pronouns have three cases: the *nominative* (used for the subject of a sentence or clause), the *objective* (used for the object of a sentence, indirect object, or object of a preposition), and the *possessive* (showing ownership). English has a different set of personal pronouns for each of these cases.

Examples

He lives here.	*He* = nominative case (subject of the sentence)
I see *him*.	*him* = objective case (object of the verb)
His car is here.	*His* = possessive case (shows ownership)

In Japanese, the personal pronouns function with all three cases, but the words stay the same. The case is shown by a *particle*, or postposition, that comes after the pronoun. Note that in the following examples of how one pronoun, *watakushi*, is used for different grammatical functions, the topic marker *wa*, rather than the subject marker *ga*, is preferred. This will be discussed in more detail in the chapter on Particles (see **§6**).

Examples

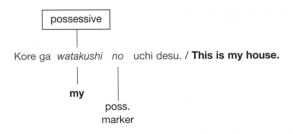

§5.3 INTERROGATIVE PRONOUNS

Although some are pronouns and some are other parts of
speech in Japanese, these are all interrogative words.

dare / **who**

dō / **how**

doko / **where** (place)

dono / **which, what**

donna / **what kind of**

donokurai / **how far, how long**

dochira / **where, which** (direction, preference)

dore / **which** (persons, things)

dotchi / **which** (of two choices)

donata / **which person, who** (polite)

dōshite / **why**

naze / **why**

nan, nani / **what**

nannin / **how many people**

ikura / **how much**

ikutsu / **how many**

itsu / **when**

§5.4 INDEFINITE PRONOUNS

dareka / **someone**	daremo / **no one**
donataka / **someone** (polite)	donatamo / **no one** (polite)
doreka / **something**	doremo / **nothing**
dokoka / **somewhere**	dokomo / **nowhere**
nanika / **something**	nanimo / **nothing**
ikuraka / **some, a little**	ikuramo / **not much**
nandemo / **anything**	nannimo / **nothing**

- Note that the expressions listed on the right side of the preceding chart take *negative* verbs in order to have a negative meaning.

Examples

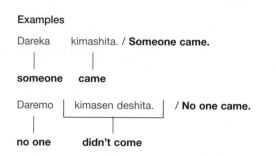

Dareka   kimashita. / **Someone came.**

someone   **came**

Daremo   kimasen deshita. / **No one came.**

no one   **didn't come**

§5.5 DEMONSTRATIVE PRONOUNS

The *demonstrative* words (some are pronouns and some are adjectives or adverbs) form a pattern of prefixes:

ko- / **here** (close to the speaker)

so- / **there** (away from the speaker)

a- / **over there** (some distance from the speaker)

do- / **question**

The last one, *do-*, can be seen in **§5.3** above.

Here are the rest:

	ko- / **here**	so- / **there**	a- / **over there**
Pronoun	kore / **this**	sore / **that**	are / **that**
Adjective	kono / **this**	sono / **that**	ano / **that**
Adjective	konna / **this kind of**	sonna / **that kind of**	anna / **that kind of**
Adverb	kō / **in this manner**	sō / **in that manner**	ā / **in that manner**
Adverb, Pronoun	koko / **here**	soko / **there**	asoko / **over there**
Adverb, Pronoun	kochira / **here, this**	sochira / **there, that**	achira / **there, that**

This form is politer usage than the one above.

§5.6 RELATIVE PRONOUNS

The *relative* pronouns in English are **who**, **whom**, **whose**, **which**, **where**, and **that**. Because relative clauses in

Japanese precede, rather than follow, the words they modify, Japanese does not have words that correspond to these pronouns.

Example

Kyō tsuita hito wa Yamada san desu. / **The man who arrived today is Mr. Yamada.**

today | man | | is
arrived | topic marker

Notice that the Japanese sentence has no word to correspond to the relative pronoun "who" in the English sentences.

This will be explained further in the section on Verbs (see **§7**).

§5.7 REFLEXIVE PRONOUNS

The *reflexive* pronouns in English are words such as **myself**, **yourself**, **himself**, **yourselves**, and so forth. Japanese has only one word to correspond to these pronouns. You might call it an all-purpose reflexive pronoun. Its meaning is both singular and plural, masculine and feminine. It can be used for humans and for warm-blooded animals. It cannot be used for fish, reptiles, insects, or inanimate objects.

> jibun / **one's self**

This is commonly followed by particles such as *de* or *no* (see **§6**).

Examples

Jibun de ikimasu. / **I'm going myself.**

Jibun de shinasai. / **Do it yourself.**

Jibun no koto wa jibun de shinasai. / **Do your own work by yourself.**

Merī san wa, jibun de benkyō shite imasu. / **Mary is studying by herself.**

§6.

Particles

§6.1 WHAT ARE PARTICLES?

A particle is a word that shows the relationship of a word, a
phrase, or a clause to the rest of the sentence. Some particles
show grammatical function—subject, object, indirect object.
Some have meaning themselves, like English prepositions. But
since they always *follow* the word or words they mark, they are
post positions.

   The lists that follow include some of the more common
particles, and some of their uses.

§6.2 PARTICLES USED WITH WORDS OR PHRASES

wa	de	made ni
ga	e	mo
o	hodo	shika
no	ka	to
ni	kara	ya
dake	made	yori

wa

topic marker

How do you decide if an expression is a topic, marked with *wa*,
or a subject, marked with *ga*? Both look like the subject of an
English sentence!

Think of the topic as a comment on something that has already been introduced into the conversation, or that is part of general or shared knowledge. As such, *wa* can mean

"Speaking of (the) . . ." or "As for (the)."

Examples

Kimura san wa, gakusei desu. / **Mr. Kimura is a student. (Speaking of Mr. Kimura, he's a student.)**

topic marker — student — is

Nihonjin wa, hashi o tsukaimasu. / **The Japanese use chopsticks. (As for the Japanese, they use chopsticks.)**

topic marker — chopsticks — obj. marker — use

- Note that *wa* as a topic marker can also follow what in English may look like an object, a phrase, or a clause.

Examples

Asagohan wa hachiji ni tabemashita. / **I ate breakfast at 8 o'clock. (Speaking of breakfast, I ate at 8 o'clock.)**

breakfast — topic marker — 8 o'clock — at — ate

Hachiji ni wa asagohan o tabemashita.

| | |
8 | at | topic | | object
o'clock | | marker | | marker

/ **I ate breakfast at 8 o'clock. (Speaking of 8 o'clock, I ate breakfast then.)**

Asagohan o tabeta no wa hachiji deshita. / **I ate breakfast at 8 o'clock. (The time I ate breakfast was 8 o'clock.)**

ate | topic marker | was

nominalizer

contrast

Wa can follow a noun to show contrast. The thing being contrasted may or may not be stated, but with this usage, the contrast is implied.

Examples

Sakana wa tabemasu ga, niku wa

| | | |
fish | eat | but | meat

tabemasen. / **I eat fish, but I don't eat meat.**

don't eat

Terebi wa | mimasen. | / **I don't watch television.**

Television   **don't watch**

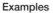

ga

subject marker

Ga marks what the Japanese call the grammatical *subject* of a sentence. Think of the subject in the following two ways:

- First, in neutral descriptions of observable actions or situations.

    Examples

Tegami ga kimashita. / **The mail came.**

mail   subj.   **came**
       marker

Ame ga | futte imasu. | / **It's raining. (The rain is falling.)**

rain   subj.   **is falling**
       marker

Note that in the negative counterparts of these sentences, *wa*, not *ga*, must be used.

   Tegami wa kimasen deshita. / **The mail didn't come.**

- Second, for special emphasis, to distinguish a particular person or thing from all others.

Examples

Watakushi ga shimashita. / **I did it. (I am the one who did it.)**

Tōkyō ga ōkii desu. / **Tokyo is big. (It is Tokyo that is big.)**

* When an interrogative pronoun is used as the subject of a sentence, *ga* must always be used too.

Example

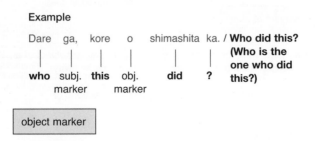

Dare   ga,   kore   o   shimashita ka. / **Who did this?**
| | | | | **(Who is the**
who   subj.   this   obj.   did   ? **one who did**
      marker   marker   **this?)**

---

object marker

O usually marks the object. But *ga* marks the object of certain non-action verbs and certain verbal adjectives and adjectival nouns (see **§8**).

Examples

Yōko san wa,   eigo   ga   wakarimasu. / **Yoko**
                                          understands
                                          English.
topic **English** obj. **understands**
marker   marker

Nihongo   ga   dekimasu ka. / **Can you speak**
                               Japanese?
          obj.   **can do?**
          marker

Hon ga hoshii desu. / **I want a book.**

book obj. **want**
marker

Merī san wa, tenisu ga jōzu desu. / **Mary is good at tennis.**

topic obj. **good at** **is**
marker marker

| o |

direct object marker

Examples

Senshū sono hon o yomimashita. / **I read that book last week.**

last week that book **read**

Jon san wa eiga o mimashita. / **John saw a movie.**

movie **saw**

through, along, in

The particle *o* is used with verbs such as **walk**, **run**, **drive**, **go through**, etc., when speaking of continuous motion and a finite place or distance.

Examples

Tanaka san wa, Chūō Dōri o arukimashita. / **Mr. Tanaka walked along Central Avenue.**

Central Avenue   walked

Kōen o hashirimashita. / **I ran through the park.**

park   ran

no

possessive marker

Think of this like the English apostrophe plus **s**.

Examples

Watakushi no inu wa, pūdoru desu. / **My dog is a poodle.**

My   dog   poodle   is

Kodomo no kao ga yogorete imasu. / **The child's face is dirty.**

Child's   face   dirty   is

noun modification

This usage of *no* is similar to the possessive, but it is seen more with compound nouns or noun phrases.

Examples

Sūgaku no kurasu wa, muzukashii desu. / **The math class is difficult.**

math   class   difficult   is

Amerika no tabemono wa, oishii desu. / **American food is delicious.**

American   food   delicious is

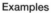

appositional

No links the noun or pronoun to the appositive that follows.

Examples

Nikuya no Doi san wa, okanemochi desu. / **The butcher, Mr. Doi, is rich.**

The butcher Mr. Doi   rich   is

Amerikajin no Jon san wa, Shikago kara

John, the American   from

kimashita. / **The American, John, is from Chicago.**

came

- For the nominalization use of *no*, see **§7.19** and **§8.5**.

ni

indirect object marker

Examples

Yamada san ni hanashimashita. / **I talked to Ms. Yamada.**

        to   talked

Hon o watakushi ni | kudasai. | / **Please give me the book. (Please give the book to me.)**

book   me   to please give

- Note that some Japanese verbs, such as **ask** and **meet**, take an indirect object, although their English counterparts do not.

Examples

Watakushi wa, Tanaka san ni kikimashita. / **I asked Mr. Tanaka.**

        to   asked

Tomodachi ni aimashita. / **I met my friend.**

friend   to   met

location

With stative (non-action) verbs meaning **there is/are**, *imasu* for people, *arimasu* for things, *ni* means **in**, **at**, or **on**, and so forth.

Examples

Merī san wa, Kyōto ni imasu. / **Mary is in Kyoto.**

Ginza wa Tōkyō ni arimasu. / **Ginza is in Tokyo.**

Haha wa depāto ni imasu. / **My mother is at the department store.**

my mother **department store**

For location, the equivalents of English expressions **near**, **under**, **inside**, **on top of**, etc. are useful. Note how they are formed in Japanese. First look at the following words:

ue / **top**	shita / **bottom**
mae / **front**	ushiro / **back**
naka / **inside**	soto / **outside**
chikaku / **nearby**	tonari / **next to**
yoko / **side**	

These words are nouns in Japanese. To form a locational phrase, the particle *no* links another noun to one of these, and then the particle *ni* follows.

tēburu   no   ue ni / **on top of the table**

table   's top on

Hon wa, tēburu no ue ni arimasu. / **The book is on top of the table.**

uchi   no   naka ni / **inside the house**

house 's inside in

Jon san wa, uchi no naka ni imasu. / **John is inside the house.**

eki   no chikaku ni / **near the station**

station 's nearby at

Yūbinkyoku wa, eki no chikaku ni arimasu. / **The post office is near the station.**

---

direction

With verbs of motion, *ni* means **to** or **toward**.

Examples

Nakamura san wa, | mainichi | Tōkyō

every day

ni ikimasu. / **Mrs. Nakamura goes to Tokyo every day.**

to goes

Ano hito | wa, Amerika ni kaerimashita. / **He returned to America.**

He   **to**   **returned**

With expressions of specific time, *ni* means **at** (clock time), **in** (month, year), or **on** (day).

Examples

> ichiji ni / **at one o'clock**
> gogo jūichiji ni / **at 11 P.M.**

Ano hitotachi | wa, | shichiji han | ni tsukimashita. / **They arrived at 7:30.**

They   **7:30**   **at**   **arrived**

> rokugatsu ni / **in June**
> kugatsu ni / **in September**
> nisenjūni nen ni / **in (the year) 2012**

Ano hito wa, shigatsu ni | umaremashita. | / **He was born in April.**

April   **in**   **was born**

Watakushi wa, 2010 nen ni Nihon ni

            | | | |

           year in Japan to

ikimashita. / **I went to Japan in 2010.**

   |

  went

getsuyōbi ni / **on Monday**

kinyōbi ni / **on Friday**

Getsuyōbi ni shigoto o hajimemasu. / **I begin work on**
                                         Monday.

  | | | |

Monday on work begin

Kayōbi ni sore o shimashō. / **Let's do it on Tuesday.**

  | | | |

Tuesday on it let's do

notion of per

Ni, is used with expressions such as **per hour**, **per day**, **per person**, etc.

Examples

ichijikan ni san doru / **three dollars per hour**

  | | | |

  hour per three dollars

Isshūkan ni yonjūhachi jikan hatarakimasu. / **I work 48 hours a week.**

| week | per | 48 | hours | work |

Sandoitchi o hitori ni futatsu tsukurimasu.

| Sandwiches | person | per | two | will make |

/ **I'll make two sandwiches per person.**

For some other uses of *ni*, see **§7.12** and **§7.13**.

dake

limitation

Dake translates English words such as **only, all, just, no more than, as many as,** and **as much as.**

Examples

Sore dake desu ka. / **Is that all?**

| that | all | is | ? |

Terebi wa, nyūsu bangumi dake mimasu. / **On television I watch only the news.**

| news | program | only | watch |

Suki na   dake   tabete   kudasai. / **Please eat as**
  | | | | **much as you**
  | | | | **want.**
want **as much as** **eat** **please**

de

place of action

This use of *de* means **in**, **at**, **on**, and so forth. It is used with action verbs, or with *arimasu* when action is implied.

Example

Panya   de   kaimashita. / **I bought it at the bakery.**
  | | |
bakery **at** **bought**

means

De translates **by**, or **by means of**, **with**, **in**, etc.

Examples

Takushī   de   ikimashita. / **I went by taxi.**
  | | |
taxi   **by**   **went**

Jisho   de   shirabemashita. / **I checked it in the**
  | | | **dictionary.**
dictionary **in** **checked**

totalizing

This use of *de* connotes a **unit**, a **certain number** or **amount**, or **together**.

Examples

futari de / **(by) two people**

Futari de shimasu. / **Two of us (together) will do it.**

		will do

Futari de shimasu. / **Two of us (together) will do it.**

```
                        will do

Nihon   ni   | futari de |   ikimasu. /  Two of us will go
  |      |        |          |              to Japan.
Japan   to   two people   will go

| Zenbu de |   sen   en   desu. /  All together it's 1,000
     |         |      |     |                    yen.
all together 1,000  yen   is
```

time limit

The meaning of *de* here is **within** or **in** for a given length of time.

Examples

```
Nishūkan     de   | dekimasu. | /  I can do it within two
   |          |         |                       weeks.
two weeks  within   can do
```

Ichijikan de ikemasu. / **You can go in one hour.**

one hour in can go

scope

Here *de* means **among**, **of**, **within**, etc., referring to extent or range.

Examples

Kudamono de, nani ga ichiban │ suki desu │ ka.

fruit of which most like ?

/ **Which of the fruit do you like the most?**

Amerika de, doko ni │ikitai desu│ ka. / **Where in**
America do
you want to
within where want to go ? **go?**

material

Here *de* means **of** or **from** in **made of** or **made from** expressions.

Examples

Kono tēburu wa, ki de │dekite imasu.│ / **This table is**
made of
wood.
table wood of is made

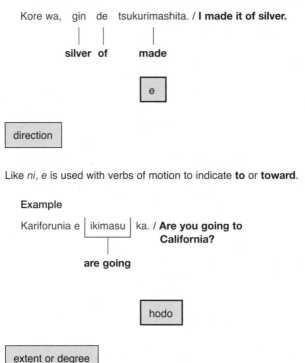

Kore wa, gin de tsukurimashita. / **I made it of silver.**

silver of made

e

direction

Like *ni*, *e* is used with verbs of motion to indicate **to** or **toward**.

Example

Kariforunia e | ikimasu | ka. / **Are you going to California?**

are going

hodo

extent or degree

Hodo means **as much as**, or **as . . . as**, and it is often used in negative constructions, although the meaning is positive.

Examples

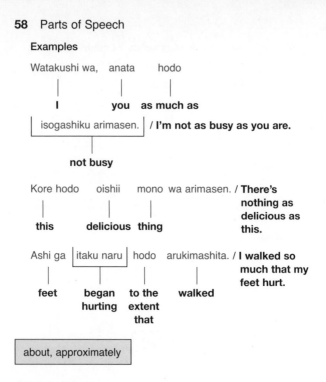

Watakushi wa, anata   hodo
| | |
I   you   as much as

isogashiku arimasen. / **I'm not as busy as you are.**
|
not busy

Kore hodo   oishii   mono wa arimasen. / **There's**
| | | **nothing as**
this   delicious thing   **delicious as**
                                             this.

Ashi ga itaku naru hodo   arukimashita. / **I walked so**
| | | | **much that my**
feet   began   to the   walked   **feet hurt.**
         hurting   extent
                     that

about, approximately

With things that can be counted, *hodo* means **about** or
approximately.

Examples

Sen   en   hodo   desu. / **It's about 1,000 yen.**
| | | |
1,000 yen about is

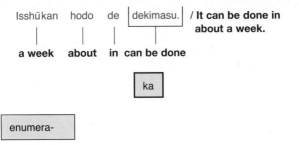

Isshūkan   hodo   de | dekimasu. | / **It can be done in about a week.**

a week   about   in   can be done

ka

enumera-

The meaning of *ka* here is **or**, that is, listing parallel things and then choosing.

Examples

Banana   ka   ringo   o   kaimashō. / **Let's buy bananas or apples.**

or   apples   let's buy

Kōhī   ka,   kōcha   ka,   kokoa wa

coffee   or   tea   or   cocoa

| ikaga desu | ka. / **Would you like coffee, tea, or cocoa?**

how about   ?

- Note that *ka*, like many particles, has several meanings. In the example above, it is also used as the question marker at the end of the sentence.

kara

place of departure, origin

The meaning of *kara* here is **from**.

Examples

Kono   kisha   wa,   Kyōto   kara   kimashita. / **This train**
  | | | | **came from**
this   train   from   came **Kyoto.**

Watakushi wa, Nihon kara kimashita. / **I am from Japan.**
  | |
I   from

starting time

The meaning of *kara* here would be expressed by **at** in
English, but in Japanese, the meaning is **from a certain time
and continuing on**. In other words, it is the beginning of a
period of time. It differs from the use of the particle *ni*, which
means **at a precise time. (Meet me at one o'clock.)**

Examples

Gēmu wa,   ichiji   kara hajimarimasu. / **The game**
  | | | | **begins**
game   one o'clock from   begins **at one**
                                   o'clock.

Getsuyōbi kara isogashiku narimasu. / **Starting Monday, I'll be busy.**

| | | | |
| Monday | from | busy | become |

source

Kara also means **from** in the sense of **origin**.

Examples

Tanaka san kara kikimashita. / **I heard it from Mrs. Tanaka.**

| | |
| from | heard |

Kono hon wa, toshokan kara karimashita. / **I borrowed this book from the library.**

| | | | | |
| this book | | library | from | borrowed |

made

target time or place

Made means **until**, **as far as**. It is often combined with *kara* in a sentence.

Example

Yūgata made benkyō shimashita. / **I studied until evening.**

| | | |
| evening | until | studied |

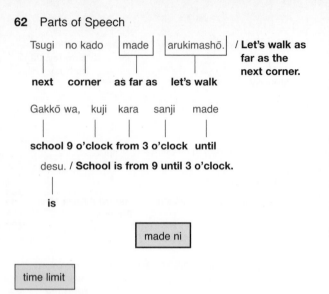

Tsugi | no kado | made | arukimashō. / **Let's walk as far as the next corner.**

next | corner | as far as | let's walk

Gakkō wa, | kuji | kara | sanji | made

school | 9 o'clock | from | 3 o'clock | until

desu. / **School is from 9 until 3 o'clock.**

is

made ni

time limit

Unlike the time limit usage of the particle *de* (**within**), *made ni* means **by** (the time given), or **not later than**.

Examples

Goji | made ni | dekimasu | ka. / **Can you do it by 5 o'clock?**

5 o'clock | by | can do

Kayōbi | made ni | hitsuyō desu. / **I need it by Tuesday.**

Tuesday | by | need

mo

including, excluding

Mo means **also** or **too**. Depending on which word it follows in a sentence, *mo* can replace *wa*, *ga*, or *o*. When used with a negative verb, the meaning is **(not) either**, or **neither . . . nor**.

Examples

Watakushi   mo | ikitai desu. | / **I want to go too.**

I   **too**   **want to go**

Gohan   mo | suki desu. | / **I also like rice.**

rice   **also**   **like**

Yōko san wa, niku   mo   sakana mo

meat   neither   fish   nor

| tabemasen. | / **Yoko eats neither meat nor fish.**

doesn't eat

emphasis

This meaning of *mo* is **even** in the sense of emphasis.

Examples

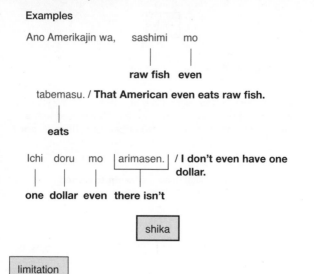

Ano Amerikajin wa,   sashimi   mo

raw fish   even

tabemasu. / **That American even eats raw fish.**

eats

Ichi   doru   mo   arimasen. / **I don't even have one dollar.**

one   dollar   even   there isn't

shika

limitation

Shika means **only, just**. Although the meaning is affirmative, it takes the negative form of the verb.

Examples

Eigo   shika   shirimasen. / **I only know English.**

English   only   don't know

Shinbun   shika   yomimasen. / **I only read newspapers.**

newspapers   only   don't read

to

complete listing

To means **and** when stating all possible items in a list. The implication is **and nothing more**.

Examples

Jon san to Merī san ga kimashita. / **John and Mary came.**

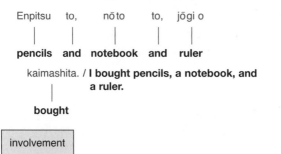

Enpitsu   to,   nō to   to,   jōgi o
| | | | |
pencils   and   notebook   and   ruler

kaimashita. / **I bought pencils, a notebook, and**
| **a ruler.**
bought

involvement

Here, *to* means **together with**.

Examples

Satō san   to   honya   e   ikimashita. / **I went to the**
| | | | **bookstore**
| | | | **with Mr. Sato.**
with bookstore to   went

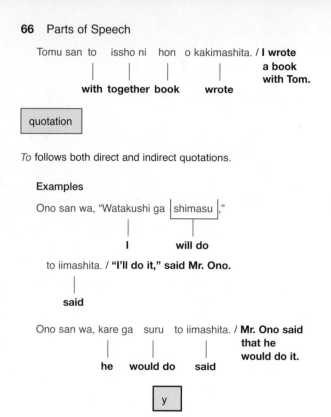

Tomu san to   issho ni   hon   o kakimashita. / **I wrote a book with Tom.**

with together book   wrote

quotation

To follows both direct and indirect quotations.

Examples

Ono san wa, "Watakushi ga | shimasu |,"

I   will do

to iimashita. / **"I'll do it," said Mr. Ono.**

said

Ono san wa, kare ga   suru   to iimashita. / **Mr. Ono said that he would do it.**

he   would do   said

y

partial listing

Ya is used for **and** when stating a sample of, or some of the items in, a list. The implication is **and others**, **among others**, or **such things as**; that is, something has been left out.

Examples

Jon san ya Merī san ga kimashita. / **John and Mary (and others) came.**

Enpitsu ya,   nōto   ya,   jōgi o
| | | | |
pencil   **and**   **notebook**   **and**   **ruler**

   kaimashita. / **I bought (such things as) a pencil, a notebook, and a ruler.**
|
bought

yori

comparison

Used when comparing things, *yori* means **than**. Think of it as the **than** in expressions such as **bigger than, smaller than, better than, worse than, rather than**, etc. It is often used in combination with *hō* (contrast) (see **§8**).

Examples

Kore   yori   sore   o kudasai. / **Please give me that rather than this.**
| | | |
this   **rather than**   **that**   **please give**

Pan   yori   gohan no hō ga
| | |
bread   **more than**   **rice**

| suki desu. | / **I like rice more than bread.**
|
like

Kyōto wa, Tōkyō yori   samui   desu. / **Kyoto is colder than Tokyo.**

| | | |
| more than | cold | is |

Amerika wa, Nihon yori   ōkii   desu. / **America is larger than Japan.**

| | | |
| more than | large | is |

§6.3 PARTICLES USED WITH CLAUSES

ga	node
kara	noni
keredo	to
nagara	

ga

contrary reasoning

Ga means **but**, or **although**. The implication is **despite the circumstances**.

Examples

Samui   desu   ga,   dekakemashita. / **Although it's cold, I went out.**

| | | | |
| cold | is | although | went out |

Byōki desu ga, shigoto ni ikimasu. / **I'm sick, but I'm going to work.**

sick am but work to go

* *Ga* is often used at the end of a clause with the final clause implied but unsaid. This has a softening effect on the exchange, with both speakers understanding the meaning of what has been left unspoken.

Examples

Ikitakatta desu ga . . . / **I wanted to go but . . . (I couldn't).**

wanted to go but

neutral connector

Here, *ga* means **and**.

Examples

Hawai ni ikimashita ga, subarashikatta desu. / **I went to Hawaii, and it was wonderful.**

went and was wonderful

Sono hon o yomimashita ga, omoshirokatta desu.

read and was interesting

/ **I read that book, and it was interesting.**

kara

reason

Here, *kara* means **because** or **since**.

Examples

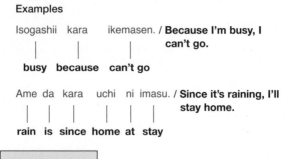

Isogashii kara ikemasen. / **Because I'm busy, I can't go.**

busy because can't go

Ame da kara uchi ni imasu. / **Since it's raining, I'll stay home.**

rain is since home at stay

sequential action

The meaning of *kara* here is **after, since, ever since**.

Examples

Tabete kara shigoto o shimasu. / **After eating, I'll do some work.**

eating after work will do

Kekkonshite kara shiawase desu. / **Ever since he got married, he has been happy.**

getting married since happy is

keredo

neutral connector

Keredo means **and**.

Examples

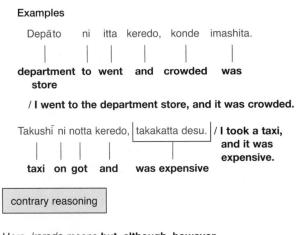

Depāto ni itta keredo, konde imashita.

| | | | | | |
| | | | | | |

department | to | went | and | crowded | was
store

/ **I went to the department store, and it was crowded.**

Takushī ni notta keredo, | takakatta desu. | / **I took a taxi,
and it was
expensive.**

taxi | on | got | and | was expensive

contrary reasoning

Here, *keredo* means **but**, **although**, **however**.

Examples

Yonda keredo, | wakarimasen deshita. | / **I read it, but I
didn't understand
it.**

read | but | didn't understand

Eiga wa omoshirokatta   keredo,

| | |

movie was interesting although

nete shimaimashita.   / **Although the movie was**
                       interesting, I fell asleep.

fell asleep

nagara

simultaneous action

Nagara means **while** or **as**.

Examples

Aruki   nagara,   hanashimashita. / **While walking, we**
                             talked.

| | |

walking while   talked

Gohan o tabe nagara, terebi o mimasu. / **As I'm eating,**
                            I watch
                            television.

| | | |

eating as   TV   watch

node

cause and effect

Node means **since** or **because** when followed by an "effect" clause.

Examples

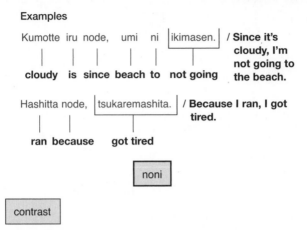

Kumotte iru node, umi ni ikimasen. / **Since it's cloudy, I'm not going to the beach.**

cloudy is since beach to not going

Hashitta node, tsukaremashita. / **Because I ran, I got tired.**

ran because got tired

noni

contrast

Noni means **in spite of** or **although**, with strong contrast between the two clauses implied.

Examples

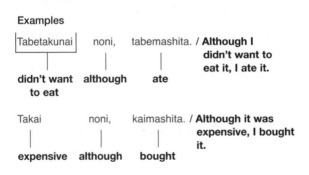

Tabetakunai noni, tabemashita. / **Although I didn't want to eat it, I ate it.**

didn't want to eat although ate

Takai noni, kaimashita. / **Although it was expensive, I bought it.**

expensive although bought

to

condition

When discussing under what condition, or under which circumstance, *to* means **if** or **when**.

Examples

Kangaeru to | wakarimasu. | / **If you think, you'll understand it.**

think if will understand

Kuji ni iku to, Sano san ni | aemasu. | / **If you go there at 9, you can see Mr. Sano.**

9 at go if can see

Tōkyō ni tsuku to, ame ga futte imashita. / **When I arrived in Tokyo, it was raining.**

arrived when rain falling was

§6.4 PARTICLES USED WITH SENTENCES

The following particles are used at the end of sentences.

question marker

Ka is like the English question mark at the end of a sentence. In Japanese, however, the word order of a statement does not change when a question is formed.

Examples

Horiguchi san wa, kirei desu. / **Mrs. Horiguchi is beautiful.**

 beautiful is

Horiguchi san wa, kirei desu ka. / **Is Mrs. Horiguchi beautiful?**

 is ?

Imōto san wa, sensei desu ka. / **Is your sister a teacher?**

sister teacher is ?

Doko de | ban gohan | o | tabetai desu | ka. / **Where do you want to eat dinner?**

where dinner want to eat ?

Itsu   eigo   o | benkyō shimashita | ka. / **When did you study English?**

when English   **studied**   **?**

ne

confirmation

Ne is similar to the English tag questions **don't you think so,** or **isn't it?** It calls for the listener to agree with or confirm what the speaker has said.

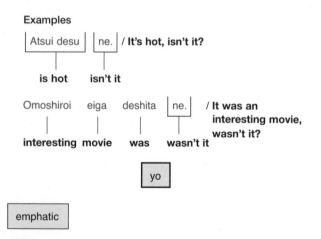

Examples

| Atsui desu | ne. | / **It's hot, isn't it?**

is hot   **isn't it**

Omoshiroi   eiga   deshita | ne. | / **It was an interesting movie, wasn't it?**

interesting movie   **was**   **wasn't it**

yo

emphatic

One usage of *yo* is similar to the English exclamation point. In that sense, it conveys emotion or strong feeling. It can also be an expression of emphasis, such as **I'm certain** (of what has just been said). Because men and women use *yo* differently, and because it can be assertive, beginners should use it with care.

Examples

Benkyō shinasai yo. / **Study!**

study

Fujisan wa, kirei desu yo. / **Mt. Fuji is beautiful!**

Mt. Fuji beautiful is !

wa

female sentence ending

Used only by women, *wa* doesn't translate easily. It can have both an emphatic function and a softening effect.

Examples

Totemo atsui wa. / **It's very hot.**

very is hot

Watakushi ga suru wa. / **I'll do it.**

will do

- In Kansai dialect, men use *wa* as an emphatic expression with different pitch from standard female usage.

> **Tip**
>
> Conjunctions in English combine words, phrases, or clauses, and can be coordinating (red *and* blue), subordinating (He stayed home *because* he was sick) or correlative (I'd like *either* coffee *or* tea). In Japanese it's different and more complex. As seen earlier in this chapter, many particles fill this function.
>
> Some examples of commonly used conjunctions follow. Although they have a combining or joining function, they are not particles because they are used only at the *beginning* of a sentence.

dakara / **so, also**
Totemo tsukarete imasu. Dakara sugu ni nemasu. / **I'm very tired. So I'll go to bed soon.**

dakedo / **but**
Sore o kaitai desu. Dakedo, totemo takai desu. / **I want to buy it. But it's very expensive.**

demo / **but**
Soko wa kirei desu. Demo tōi desu. / **It's beautiful there. But it's far.**

sarani / **furthermore**
Tomu san wa Supeingo to Furansugo o hanashimasu. Sarani, Nihongo to Chūgokugo mo hanashimasu. / **Tom speaks Spanish and French. Furthermore, he speaks Japanese and Chinese too.**

sonoue / **besides, furthermore**

Restoran wa totemo takai deshita. Sonoue, oishiku arimasen
    deshita. / **The restaurant was very expensive. Besides,
    the food was not delicious.**

sorekara / **and then, then**

Kōhī o nomimashita. Sorekara kēki o tabemashita. / **I drank
    coffee. And then I ate cake.**

soshite / **and, also**

Jon san wa Nihon ni ikimashita. Soshite Nihongo o benkyō
    shimashita. / **John went to Japan. And he studied
    Japanese.**

soretomo / **or**

Pan ga tabetai desu ka. Soretomo gohan ga tabetai desu ka. /
    Do you want to eat bread? Or do you want to eat rice?

§7.

Verbs

§7.1 WHAT ARE VERBS?

Verbs are words that describe an action, a process, or a state of being.

Verbs have different forms which enable you to express time, intention, feelings, politeness, etc. Japanese verbs express these things too, but in different ways from those of English and other Indo-European languages. As you have seen in **§3**, for example, the main verb of a Japanese sentence must be at the end. In this section, you will see other differences, as well as some similarities.

§7.2 AGREEMENT

In English a verb must agree with its subject in person and number. In the present tense, for example, a subject in the first person takes a different verb form from a subject in the third person. And a plural subject in the third person takes a different verb form from a singular subject.

Examples

Person	Singular	Plural
First Person	**I go**	**we go**
Second Person	**you go**	**you go**
Third Person	**he/she/it goes**	**they go**

- In Japanese, agreement is not an issue. Verbs do not have different forms to indicate person, number, or gender. The *same* verb form is used no matter what the subject. This is true for all tenses.

Examples

Person	Singular	Plural
First Person	ikimasu / **I go**	ikimasu / **we go**
Second Person	ikimasu / **you go**	ikimasu / **you go**
Third Person	ikimasu / **he/she/ it goes**	ikimasu / **they go**

Tip	This principle is easy to understand if you remember the following: If the meaning is clear from the context in a Japanese sentence, a pronoun is not necessary. Therefore, *Ikimasu* is both a verb and a sentence.

- In English, except for the imperative, or command form, a sentence consisting of a verb alone is not possible.

§7.3 VERB CONJUGATIONS

Japanese verbs can be classified into two major groups, or conjugations. The only exceptions are two irregular verbs: *suru*, **to do**, and *kuru*, **to come**.

These groupings are a basic key to the Japanese verb system. They enable you to change the verb forms for different tenses and moods.

In a dictionary, an English verb is listed in its infinitive, or **to** form: **(to) go**, **(to) see**, etc. A Japanese verb, on the other hand, is listed in what is called its "dictionary form." The dictionary form is the basis for categorizing a verb into one of the two major conjugations.

The two groups differ in how they form their stems and their infinitives. The stem is the most important inflectional base, which may change, or to which different suffixes, or endings, are added, to show tense, mood, and politeness level. The infinitive is the second most important inflectional base.

§7.3–1   The Consonant Conjugation

> In this group, the verb stems end in a consonant. Therefore, they may be called **c-stem** verbs, as we shall do here. Because the stems are formed by dropping the final **u**, this is also referred to as the **u-dropping conjugation**, and the verbs may be called **u-dropping verbs**.

> How can you tell a Consonant Conjugation verb?

- If the dictionary form ends in anything but -*eru* or -*iru*, it belongs in this group.

> How do you form the stem?

- To form the stem of the verb, drop the final -*u*.

Examples

DICTIONARY FORM	STEM	ENGLISH
isogu	isog-	**to hurry**
kaku	kak-	**to write**
kiku	kik-	**to ask**
tobu	tob-	**to fly**
shinu	shin-	**to die**
yomu	yom-	**to read**

- For a few verbs, certain sound changes are necessary:

  If a verb ends in -*su*, the stem ends in *sh* before a suffix beginning with *i*, or *s* before other suffixes.

  If a verb ends in -*tsu*, the stem ends in *ch* before a suffix beginning with *i*, or *t* before other suffixes. For example:

DICTIONARY FORM	STEM	ENGLISH
dasu	das- dash-	**to take out**
kasu	kas- kash-	**to lend**
matsu	mat- mach-	**to wait**
tatsu	tat- tach-	**to stand**

If a verb ends in *-au*, *-iu*, or *-ou*, it is still considered a
c-stem verb, and it belongs in this group, even though a
vowel remains after the *u* is dropped. The reason is that a
missing "*w*" is considered the final consonant of the
stem. That *w*, although not used in the affirmative forms,
is needed for some of the negative forms. For example:

DICTIONARY FORM	STEM	ENGLISH
shimau	shima(w)-	to put away
kau	ka(w)-	to buy
iu	i(w)-	to say
omou	omo(w)-	to think

- Some verbs that end in *-eru* and *-iru* belong to the c-stem
verb group. Here are a few examples:

DICTIONARY FORM	STEM	ENGLISH
hairu	hair-	to enter
kaeru	kaer-	to return
shiru	shir-	to know
kiru	kir-	to cut
iru	ir-	to need

Note that *kiru*, **to cut**, is a c-stem verb. When pronounced,
the first syllable is stressed. The verb *kiru*, **to wear**, is a
v-stem verb (see **§7.3–2** and **§22**). When pronounced, the
second syllable is stressed.

§7.3–2 The Vowel Conjugation

In this group, the verb stems end in a vowel. Therefore, they may be called **v-stem** verbs, as we shall do here. Because the stems are formed by dropping the final **ru**, this is also referred to as the **ru-dropping conjugation**, and the verbs may be called **ru-dropping verbs**.

How can you tell a Vowel Conjugation verb?

- Most verbs with dictionary forms which end in *-eru* and *-iru* belong in this group. (For some exceptions, see **§7.3–1**.)

How do you form the stem?

- To form the stem of the verb, drop the final *-ru*.

Examples

DICTIONARY FORM	STEM	ENGLISH
ageru	age-	to give, to raise
dekiru	deki-	to be able
hajimeru	hajime-	to begin
iru	i-	to be
kangaeru	kangae-	to think
miru	mi-	to see
neru	ne-	to sleep
taberu	tabe-	to eat
kiru	ki-	to wear

§7.4 THE INFINITIVE

The infinitive is also an important base for constructing other verb forms. To form the infinitive, do the following:

- for c-stem verbs, add *-i* to the stem. For example:

DICTIONARY FORM	STEM	INFINITIVE
isogu	isog-	isogi-
kaku	kak-	kaki-
kiku	kik-	kiki-
tobu	tob-	tobi-
shinu	shin-	shini-
yomu	yom-	yomi-

- for v-stem verbs, add *nothing* to the stem. (In this conjugation, the stem and the infinitive are the same.) For example:

DICTIONARY FORM	STEM	INFINITIVE
ageru	age-	age-
dekiru	deki-	deki-
hajimeru	hajime-	hajime-
iru	i-	i-
kangaeru	kangae-	kangae-
miru	mi-	mi-

- For the irregular verbs, the forms are as follows:

DICTIONARY FORM	INFINITIVE
kuru	ki-
suru	shi-

§7.5 PLAIN AND POLITE FORMS

The Japanese use different sets, or levels, of verb forms, depending on the politeness requirements of the situation, and the relationship among the speakers. For non-Japanese, using the different politeness levels correctly takes a great deal of experience with the Japanese language and culture.

The two most common levels are called *plain* and *polite*. The plain verb forms are used with immediate family members and close friends and associates. The polite forms have a wider range, and are more appropriate for general use, especially for students of Japanese.

The examples below show two ways of saying the same thing, one plain style, and one polite style. Note the different verb forms.

Plain	Present Past	da / dictionary form datta / -ta, -da
Polite	Present Past	desu / -masu deshita / -mashita

- Both plain and polite forms are introduced with new verbs throughout this chapter.

Examples

plain form

PLAIN SENTENCE	Ban gohan	o tabeta. / **I ate dinner.**

dinner   **ate**

polite form

POLITE SENTENCE	Ban gohan	o tabemashita. / **I ate dinner.**

dinner   **ate**

Tip	Although readers of this book should use the polite level, both forms must be learned. This is because the plain form can function other than as the main verb. When the main verb of the sentence, the one at the end, is in the polite form, other verbs earlier in the same sentence usually take the plain form.

The following examples show two sentences that say the same thing, one plain style, the other polite. Note that both sentences use a plain verb form, *tabeta*, for **ate**. And keep in mind that the verb at the end determines the politeness level for the entire sentence.

Examples

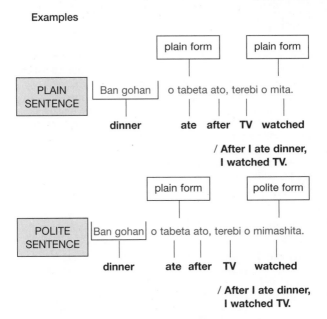

/ **After I ate dinner, I watched TV.**

/ **After I ate dinner, I watched TV.**

In the sections on verbs that follow, both the plain and polite forms will be given. Although there are other, more formal verb forms, these two levels should be appropriate for the reader's needs.

§7.6 THE "TO BE" VERBS

English has one verb to express the meaning **to be**, although that verb takes several forms (**am**, **is**, **are**, **was**, **were**, etc.). Japanese has three different words, each expressing a particular aspect of the meaning of **to be**: *desu*, *arimasu*, and *imasu*.

desu

Often called the copula, *desu* is used when you want to indicate such things as condition, quality, number, characteristics, or identity. You can understand it more easily if you think of *desu* as meaning not only **is**, but also **equals**, especially with two nouns or noun phrases. If you can substitute **equals** for **is** in an English sentence such as **This equals/is a book** or **Mrs. Smith equals/is my best friend**, *desu* is the word you want.

Although the polite forms *desu* (present) and *deshita* (past) are the ones you will use most often, you should know the following forms as well.

desu / **is, equals**		**Affirmative**	**Negative**
Present	Plain	da	dewa nai
	Polite	desu	dewa arimasen
Past	Plain	datta	dewa nakatta
	Polite	deshita	dewa arimasen deshita
Probable	Plain	darō	dewa nai darō
	Polite	deshō	dewa nai deshō

• For informal or familiar usage, *ja* can replace *dewa*.

Examples

Kore wa, hon desu. / **This is a book.**

this book is

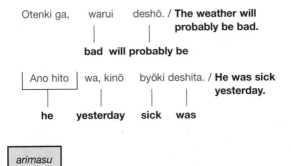

Tanaka san wa, sensei desu. / **Mr. Tanaka is a teacher.**

teacher

Otenki ga, ii desu. / **The weather is good.**

weather good

Otenki ga, warui deshō. / **The weather will probably be bad.**

bad will probably be

Ano hito wa, kinō byōki deshita. / **He was sick yesterday.**

he yesterday sick was

---

arimasu

Arimasu means **is** or **exists** for the location of inanimate things. It also expresses the idea of English **to have**. If you think of the meaning as **(something) exists/is located (somewhere)**, *arimasu* is the word you want. Because *arimasu* is a stative (non-action) verb, the particle *ni* is used with expressions of location.

Example

Hon wa, tēburu no ue ni arimasu. / **The book is on the table.**

table 's top on

In the **to have** meaning of *arimasu*, the thing possessed is the subject of the sentence, and takes the particle *ga*.

Examples

Okane ga arimasu ka. / **Do you have any money?**

money   is   **(As for you, does money exist?)**

Hai, arimasu. / **Yes, I do. (Yes, it exists.)**

yes

Here are the other forms of arimasu:

arimasu / is, exists		Affirmative	Negative
Present	Plain	aru	nai
	Polite	arimasu	arimasen
Past	Plain	atta	nakatta
	Polite	arimashita	arimasen deshita
Probable	Plain	aru darō	nai darō
	Polite	aru deshō	nai deshō

Examples

Fujisan wa, Nihon ni arimasu. / **Mt. Fuji is in Japan.**

in   is

Ginza ni, sūpā ga arimasu ka. / **Is there a supermarket in Ginza?**

|
supermarket

Eki wa, doko ni arimasu ka. / **Where is the station?**

| |
station where

Jisho ga arimasu ka. / **Do you have a dictionary?**

|
dictionary

Iie, arimasen. / **No, I don't (have a dictionary).**

Koko ni kōen ga arimashita. / **There was a park here.**

| | |
here park was

---

imasu

Imasu is also a stative (non-action) verb used to express **is** or **exists** for location. But *imasu* is used for living things— people, animals, insects (*not* plants). The particle *ni* is used with *imasu* when the location is specified.

Imasu is also used as an auxiliary verb to form the pro- gressive tenses, where it functions just like the English **is**: **He is going, I was going,** etc. Because this meaning of *imasu* is discussed in **§7.7–4** and **§7.7–5**, the examples below will deal with only the locational meaning. First, here are the other forms of *imasu*:

imasu / **is, exists**		**Affirmative**	**Negative**
Present	Plain	iru	inai
	Polite	imasu	imasen
Past	Plain	ita	inakatta
	Polite	imashita	imasen deshita
Probable	Plain	iru darō	inai darō
	Polite	iru deshō	inai deshō

Examples

Tanaka san wa imasu ka. / **Is Mr. Tanaka here?**

Hai, imasu. / **Yes, he is.**

Kinō Tōkyō ni imashita ka. / **Were you in Tokyo yesterday?**

yesterday   **were**

Neko wa doko ni imasu ka. / **Where is the cat?**

cat   **where**

Merī san wa, | raigetsu | Nihon ni

next month

| iru deshō. | / **Mary will probably be in Japan next month.**

will probably be

§7.7 THE INDICATIVE MOOD

The indicative mood allows you to express ordinary, objective statements, questions, etc. Tense refers to the time of the action or state expressed by the verb.

Tip	Sometimes Japanese is described as having just two tenses: the past and the non-past. At first, this sounds strange; on second thought, it can be a useful concept. What does it mean? It means that *Japanese does not have a separate future tense*. The past is the past, the non-past is everything else—that is, present and future. Here we will use more conventional terms (present and past), however.

Keep in mind as you look at the different tenses and moods that Japanese verbs do not change their form for gender and number.

§7.7–1 Present Tense

The present tense meanings in Japanese are similar to those of English: incomplete or habitual actions or states. The present tense is used for future time as well; Japanese has no separate future tense.

The plain form of the present tense is the same as the dictionary form, the one from which the stem is derived. The dictionary form was discussed in **§7.3**, Verb Conjugations.

> plain form, c-stem verbs (see **§7.3–1**)

iku /   **I go, you go, he/she/it goes, we go, they go, I will go, you will go, he/she/it will go, we will go, they will go**

yomu /   **I read, you read, he/she/it reads, we read, they read, I will read, you will read, he/she/it will read, we will read, they will read**

> plain form, v-stem verbs (see **§7.3–1**)

miru /   **I see, you see, he/she/it sees, we see, they see, I will see, you will see, he/she/it will see, we will see, they will see**

taberu /   **I eat, you eat, he/she/it eats, we eat, they eat, I will eat, you will eat, he/she/it will eat, we will eat, they will eat**

- To form the negative of the plain form, do the following:

> c-stem verbs: add *-anai* to the stem.

iku / ikanai	**go / don't go**
yomu / yomanai	**read / don't read**

- Note that for c-stem verbs ending in *-au*, *-iu*, or *-ou*, you must add a *w* to the stem before adding *-anai* (see **§7.3–1**).

shimau / shimawanai	**put away / don't put away**
kau / kawanai	**buy / don't buy**
iu / iwanai	**say / don't say**
omou / omowanai	**think / don't think**

v-stem verbs: add -*nai* to the stem

hajimeru / hajimenai	**begin / don't begin**
kangaeru / kangaenai	**think / don't think**
taberu / tabenai	**eat / don't eat**
ageru / agenai	**give / don't give**
miru / minai	**see / don't see**

Tip The polite present is sometimes referred to as the *masu* form. It can be constructed in two different ways.

Either: Add -*masu* to the infinitive. (See **§7.4**.)

c-stem verbs	isogi + masu	isogimasu / **hurry**
	kaki + masu	kakimasu / **write**
	kiki + masu	kikimasu / **ask**
	tobi + masu	tobimasu / **fly**
	shini + masu	shinimasu / **die**
	yomi + masu	yomimasu / **read**
v-stem verbs	age + masu	agemasu / **give**
	hajime + masu	hajimemasu / **begin**
	kangae + masu	kangaemasu / **think about**
	mi + masu	mimasu / **see**
	ki + masu	kimasu / **wear**
	ori + masu	orimasu / **get off**

Or:	For c-stem verbs, add *-imasu* to the stem.

isogu isog + imasu	isogimasu / **hurry**
kaku kak + imasu	kakimasu / **write**
kiku kik + imasu	kikimasu / **ask**

For v-stem verbs, add *-masu* to the stem.

hajimeru hajime + masu	hajimemasu / **begin**
kangaeru kangae + masu	kangaemasu / **think about**
miru mi + masu	mimasu / **see**

• To form the polite negative, do the following:

For all verbs, simply change the ending from *masu* to *masen*.

ikimasu / ikimasen	**go / don't go**
wakarimasu / wakarimasen	**understand / don't understand**
kakimasu / kakimasen	**write / don't write**
mimasu / mimasen	**see / don't see**
oshiemasu / oshiemasen	**teach / don't teach**

Here are a few verbs in their present tense conjugations:

Verb	Affirmative	Negative
taberu / **eat** Present Plain Polite	taberu tabemasu	tabenai tabemasen
nomu / **drink** Present Plain Polite	nomu nomimasu	nomanai nomimasen
suru / **do** Present Plain Polite	suru shimasu	shinai shimasen

And some present tense sentences:

Examples

Watakushi wa, kōhī o | nomimasen. | / **I don't drink coffee.**

        coffee   **don't drink**

Tanaka san wa, mainichi sushi o tabemasu. / **Mr. Tanaka eats sushi every day.**

        every day   **eats**

Ano hitotachi | wa, terebi o   mimasen. / **They don't watch television.**

  they   **television**   **don't watch**

Nihongo ga wakarimasu ka. / **Do you understand Japanese?**

| understand

Ashita Kyōto ni ikimasu. / **I'll go to Kyoto tomorrow.**

tomorrow **will go**

§7.7–2 Past Tense

Like English, the past tense is used for actions completed in the past (**I ate, I studied**, etc.). It is also used to express the equivalent of the English present perfect (**I have walked, I have eaten**, etc.).

Forming the plain past tense is easy for v-stem verbs, more complex for c-stem verbs.

> For plain form, v-stem verbs: add *-ta* to the stem.

taberu / tabeta	**eat / ate**
oshieru / oshieta	**teach / taught**
miru / mita	**see / saw**
ageru / ageta	**give / gave**

> For plain form, c-stem verbs: do the following:

- Look at the *final* syllable in the plain present form (dictionary form) of the verb. Find the syllable in column A below. Change it to the syllable in column B.

A	B

change this ⟶ to this	
omou	u ⟶ tta	omotta / **thought**
motsu	tsu ⟶ tta	motta / **held**
toru	ru ⟶ tta	totta / **took**
nomu	mu ⟶ nda	nonda / **drank**
shinu	nu ⟶ nda	shinda / **died**
tobu	bu ⟶ nda	tonda / **flew**
kiku	ku ⟶ ita	kiita / **asked**
oyogu	gu ⟶ ida	oyoida / **swam**
hanasu	su ⟶ shita	hanashita / **talked**

- To form the negative of the plain past tense, do the following:

> c-stem verbs: add -*anakatta* to the stem

iku	itta / ikanakatta	**went / didn't go**
yomu	yonda / yomanakatta	**read / didn't read**
kau(w)	katta / kawanakatta	**bought / didn't buy**
isogu	isoida / isoganakatta	**hurried / didn't hurry**

> v-stem verbs: add -*nakatta* to the stem.

hajimeru	hajimeta / hajimenakatta	**began / didn't begin**
taberu	tabeta / tabenakatta	**ate / didn't eat**
ageru	ageta / agenakatta	**gave / didn't give**
miru	mita / minakatta	**saw / didn't see**

For the polite past tense, change the present tense ending from *masu* to *mashita*.

ikimasu / ikimashita	**go / went**
mimasu / mimashita	**see / saw**
kaimasu / kaimashita	**buy / bought**
wakarimasu / wakarimashita	**understand / understood**
tabemasu / tabemashita	**eat / ate**
shimasu / shimashita	**do / did**
kimasu / kimashita	**come / came**

• For the negative of the polite past, add the word *deshita* to the polite present negative.

tabemasen / tabemasen deshita	**don't eat / didn't eat**
ikimasen / ikimasen deshita	**don't go / didn't go**
hashirimasen / hashirimasen deshita	**don't run / didn't run**
kaimasen / kaimasen deshita	**don't buy / didn't buy**

Here are a few verbs in their past tense conjugations:

Verb	Affirmative	Negative
kiru / **to put on (clothes)**		
Past Plain	kita	kinakatta
Polite	kimashita	kimasen deshita
yomu / **to read**		
Past Plain	yonda	yomanakatta
Polite	yomimashita	yomimasen deshita
suru / **to do**		
Past Plain	shita	shinakatta
Polite	shimashita	shimasen deshita

And some past tense sentences:

Examples

Itsu kimashita ka. / **When did you come?**

| |
when came

Kinō | shimasen deshita. | / **I didn't do it yesterday.**

yesterday   didn't do

Owarimashita. / **It's finished.**

finished

Doko de kaimashita ka. / **Where did you buy it?**

bought

Naze | ikimasen deshita | ka. / **Why didn't you go?**

why   didn't go

§7.7–3   The Gerund

Often referred to as the "-*te* form," the gerund is a useful form of the Japanese verb. Alone, it does not have tense or mood. But it combines with other verb forms to create tenses and moods, such as the continuous tenses and the imperative mood, for example. It has other uses as well.

Tip	One caution: The term "gerund" may be misleading. In English, a gerund is the **-ing** form of a verb when functioning as a noun (**I like swimming, Reading is my favorite hobby**, etc. For this use, see **§7.19**). The Japanese gerund is a verb form, *not* a noun. Indeed, in the progressive tenses, it functions much like the English **-ing** form.

Gerunds are regular in form and easy to construct.

Start with the plain past tense (see **§7.7–2**), and change the final -*a* to -*e*.

Present	Past	Gerund
aruku / **walk**	aruita	aruite
kiku / **ask, listen**	kiita	kiite
taberu / **eat**	tabeta	tabete
hanasu / **speak**	hanashita	hanashite
yomu / **read**	yonda	yonde

Note that for the copula, *desu*, the plain past tense is *datta* and the gerund is *de*.

One important use of the gerund is when listing actions in a neutral sequence (with no strong contrast or emphasis) within a sentence. All but the last verb are gerunds.

Example

Sūpā ni itte, niku o katte, uchi ni

went	**meat**	**bought**

kaerimashita. / **I went to the supermarket, bought**
                some meat, and returned home.

returned

§7.7–4 Present Progressive

Japanese uses the present progressive for action in progress or continuous action, state of being, and also to express the meaning of the English present perfect.

Unlike English, it cannot be used to express future meaning (**Tomorrow he's going to New York**, or **I'm getting my degree next year**, etc.).

To form the present progressive, start with the gerund, and add the appropriate form of the verb *iru*. The plain form is used in informal conversation, of course. The polite form, appropriate for general use, is given here. Note that *iru* when used alone as a verb can only refer to living things. With the gerund, it is used for inanimate things as well.

Affirmative	Negative
aruite imasu / **walking**	aruite imasen / **not walking**
kiite imasu / **listening**	kiite imasen / **not listening**
tabete imasu / **eating**	tabete imasen / **not eating**
hanashite imasu / **speaking**	hanashite imasen / **not speaking**
yonde imasu / **reading**	yonde imasen / **not reading**
nonde imasu / **drinking**	nonde imasen / **not drinking**
motte imasu / **holding**	motte imasen / **not holding**
oyoide imasu / **swimming**	oyoide imasen / **not swimming**

When the meaning of this tense is an action in progress, the verb is often transitive (a verb that takes an object). This is similar to the English present progressive.

Examples

Ima, ban gohan o | tabete imasu. / **I'm eating dinner now.**

now | am eating

Nani o | shite imasu ka. / **What are you doing?**

what | are doing

Eigo o | benkyō shite imasu. / **I'm studying English.**

am studying

Tegami o | kaite imasu. / **I'm writing a letter.**

letter | am writing

When the meaning is a state of being, the verb is often intransitive (a verb that doesn't take an object). This is not like an English progressive tense usage; the explanations after the examples below should help clarify the meanings.

Examples

Mado ga | aite imasu. / **The window is open. (Someone opened it, and it's still open.)**

window | is open

Mise ga | shimatte imasu. / **The store is closed.
(Someone closed it,
and it's still closed.)**

store | is closed

Ano hito | wa | futotte imasu. / **He is fat. (He got fat,
and he's still fat.)**

he | is fat

Haha wa Tōkyō ni | itte imasu. / **Mother is in Tokyo.
(She went to Tokyo,
and she's still there.)**

mother | is

Tsukarete imasu. / **I'm tired. (I got tired, and
I'm still tired.)**

tired

The present progressive can express the English present perfect tense—an action that began in the past and continues through the present. In the following sentences, notice how the time element, **for five years**, results in a present perfect meaning. Without it, the meaning is simply continuous action.

Examples

Kyōto ni gonen kan | sunde imasu. / **I have been
living in Kyoto
for five years.**

five years for | am living

Kyōto ni sunde imasu. / **I'm living in Kyoto.**

§7.7–5 Past Progressive

The past progressive is used for past continuous action or state of being.

> The form is easy: start with the gerund, and change *imasu* to the past form: *imashita*. The negative is the gerund plus the negative past of *imashita*, which is *imasen deshita*.

Affirmative	Negative
aruite imashita / **was walking**	aruite imasen deshita / **wasn't walking**
kiite imashita / **was listening**	kiite imasen deshita / **wasn't listening**
tabete imashita / **was eating**	tabete imasen deshita / **wasn't eating**
hanashite imashita / **was speaking**	hanashite imasen deshita / **wasn't speaking**
yonde imashita / **was reading**	yonde imasen deshita / **wasn't reading**
nonde imashita / **was drinking**	nonde imasen deshita / **wasn't drinking**
motte imashita / **was holding**	motte imasen deshita / **wasn't holding**
oyoide imashita / **was swimming**	oyoide imasen deshita / **wasn't swimming**

Here are some examples of past continuous action.

Examples

Haha wa, ban gohan o | tsukutte imashita. | / **Mother was preparing dinner.**

was making

Chichi wa, | hataraite imasen deshita. | / **Father wasn't working.**

father   **wasn't working**

Kyonen Nihongo o | benkyō shite imashita. | / **Last year I was studying Japanese.**

last year   **was studying**

Neko ga, | isu no | ue de | nete imashita. | / **The cat was sleeping on the chair.**

cat   **chair's** **top**   **was sleeping**

The following examples show past states of being.

Examples

Denki ga | tsuite imashita. | / **The light was on.**

light   **was on**

Doa ga | aite imashita. | / **The door was open.**

door   **was open**

Ano hito wa | yasete imashita. | / **She was thin.**

was thin

Tsukarete imasen deshita. / **I wasn't tired.**

tired

§7.8 THE PRESUMPTIVE MOOD

Sometimes called the "probable" mood, this has no exact equivalent in English, although it is important in Japanese. It enables speakers to use a verb form that can express *probability*, *belief*, or *intention* without being too direct. This mood has two sets of forms, one indicating probability, the second indicating intention.

> *darō, deshō* form

This form expresses the speaker's belief that something will probably happen. It is easily constructed by adding *darō* or *deshō* (plain and polite, respectively) to the plain, or dictionary form, of the verb. This works for the negative of the plain form as well, and also for the past forms.

Present	
Plain	**Polite**
kuru darō	kuru deshō / **will probably come**
iku darō	iku deshō / **will probably go**
taberu darō	taberu deshō / **will probably eat**
Negative	
konai darō	konai deshō / **will probably not come**
ikanai darō	ikanai deshō / **will probably not go**
tabenai darō	tabenai deshō / **will probably not eat**
Past	
kita darō	kita deshō / **probably came**
itta darō	itta deshō / **probably went**
tabeta darō	tabeta deshō / **probably ate**
Negative	
konakatta darō	konakatta deshō / **probably didn't come**
ikanakatta darō	ikanakatta deshō / **probably didn't go**
tabanakatta darō	tabenakatta deshō / **probably didn't eat**

The examples below show some expanded dimensions of these forms, which can also be translated as **suppose**, **wonder**, **guess**, etc.

Examples

Ano hito wa, Nihon ni | iku deshō. | / He'll probably go
to Japan.

will probably go

Konban yuki ga | furu darō. | / Tonight it will
probably snow.

tonight snow will probably fall

Merī san wa, Nihon de Nihongo o

Japan in Japanese

hanashita deshō ka. | / I wonder if Mary spoke
Japanese in Japan.

wonder if spoke

Jon san wa, | tsukareta deshō. | / I suppose John got
tired.

suppose got tired

Yūbin wa, jūji ni | kuru deshō. | / I guess the mail will
come at 10.

mail 10 at guess will come

> *-ō, -yō / -mashō forms*

These differ somewhat in the plain and polite forms.

First consider the plain form, *-ō, -yō*. As a final verb at the end of a sentence, it expresses the speaker's intention. Considered abrupt, it is used mostly by men. It can also mean "Let's (do something)," but for this, the *-mashō* form is preferred. As a medial verb (not at the end of the sentence), it expresses intention or probability. The forms are made as follows:

- For c-stem verbs, start with the plain, or dictionary form, and change the final *-u* to *-ō*.

Present	Presumptive
kau / **buy**	kaō / **will probably buy, will/let's buy**
kiku / **ask**	kikō / **will probably ask, will/let's ask**

- For v-stem verbs, start with the stem, and add *-yō*.

Present	Stem	Presumptive
taberu / **eat**	tabe-	tabeyō / **will probably eat, will/let's eat**
miru / **see**	mi-	miyō / **will probably see, will/let's see**

- The irregular verb forms are as follows:

suru / **do**	shiyō / **will probably do, will/let's do**
kuru / **come**	koyō / **will probably come, will/let's come**

- The negative forms, infrequently used, are not needed here.
- Note how the ō and yō forms are used in medial and final position, and the differences in meaning.

Examples

Konban hayaku   neyō

tonight   early   probably go to sleep

    to   omoimasu. / **I think I'll probably go to sleep early tonight.**

that   think

Watakushi ga ikō. / **I will go.**

will go

Tabeyō. / **Let's eat.**

Now look at the polite form, -*mashō*. This can express several things: the speaker's intention to do something, a polite description of the probability of someone else's doing something, or, most common, the idea of "Let's" or "Shall we?"

To construct this form, add *-mashō* to the infinitive of the verb.

Plain	Infinitive	*-mashō* Form
yomu / **read**	yomi-	yomimashō / **let's read**
miru / **see**	mi-	mimashō / **let's see**
taberu / **eat**	tabe-	tabemashō / **let's eat**
iku / **go**	iki-	ikimashō / **let's go**

Here are some examples of some common uses of this form:

Examples

Ginza ni ikimashō. / **Let's go to Ginza.**

let's go

| Ban gohan | o | tabemashō ka. | / **Shall we eat dinner?**

dinner   **shall we eat**

Uchi ni | kaerimashō. | / **Let's return home.**

home   **let's return**

Watakushi ga shimashō. / **I'll do it.**

will do

Jon san ga kimashō. / **John will probably come.**

will probably come

* Note that the last sentence above would mean the same thing using the *deshō* form. For example:

Jon san ga | kuru deshō. | / **John will probably come.**

will probably come.

§7.9 THE IMPERATIVE MOOD

The true imperative or command form in Japanese is too abrupt for most usage. However, you should recognize it.

The imperative is formed by adding *-e* to the stem of c-stem verbs, and *-ro* to the stem of v-stem verbs. To form the negative imperatives, add *-na* to the plain present form of the verb.

Plain	Imperative	Imperative (Negative)
iku / **go**	ike / **go!**	ikuna / **don't go!**
kiku / **listen**	kike / **listen!**	kikuna / **don't listen!**
taberu / **eat**	tabero / **eat!**	taberuna / **don't eat!**
miru / **look**	miro / **look!**	miruna / **don't look!**

A somewhat less harsh form is made by adding -*nasai* to the infinitive form of the verb. This is not used with negative forms.

iku / **go**	ikinasai / **go**
taberu / **eat**	tabenasai / **eat**

Examples

Yukkuri hanashinasai. / **Speak slowly.**

| |
slowly   speak

Koko ni kinasai. / **Come here.**

| |
here   come

The form of the imperative commonly used for polite requests or commands is the gerund, or -*te* form, with the word *kudasai*.

kuru / **come**	Kite kudasai. / **Please come.**
taberu / **eat**	Tabete kudasai. / **Please eat.**
suwaru / **sit down**	Suwatte kudasai. / **Please sit down.**
kiku / **listen**	Kiite kudasai. / **Please listen.**
hanasu / **speak**	Hanashite kudasai. / **Please speak.**

Examples

Ryokō ni tsuite | hanashite kudasai. / **Please tell me about your trip.**

trip   about   please tell

Tegami o | dashite kudasai. | / **Please mail the letter.**

letter   please mail

Takushī o | yonde kudasai. | / **Please call a taxi.**

taxi   please call

For the negative of this structure, add *-de kudasai* to the negative of the plain present form.

Ikanaide kudasai. / **Please don't go.**
Shinpai shinaide kusasai. / **Please don't worry.**

Kudasai can also be used when requesting an object. In this usage another verb form is not needed.

Examples

Hon o   kudasai. / **Please give me a book.**

book   please give

Kōhī o   kudasai. / **Please give me some coffee.**

coffee please give

§7.10 THE CONDITIONAL MOOD

In Japanese, there are several ways of conveying the conditional, or "if" meaning. Although they can, in many cases, be used interchangeably, there are slight differences in meaning.

-eba form

This is sometimes called the "provisional" form, because it means "if" in the sense of "provided something happens (now or in the future)." In the negative form, it can mean "unless."

For the -eba form, drop the final -u of the dictionary form of the verb and add -eba. For the negative, drop the final -i of the plain negative form and add -kereba.

Plain	Conditional
kuru / **come**	kureba / **if, provided I (you, etc.) come** konakereba / **if I don't come, unless I come**
miru / **see**	mireba / **if, provided I see** minakereba / **if I don't see, unless I see**
yomu / **read**	yomeba / **if, provided I read** yomanakereba / **if I don't read, unless I read**
taberu / **eat**	tabereba / **if, provided I eat** tabenakereba / **if I don't eat, unless I eat**

Examples

Isshōkenmei | benkyō sureba, | Nihongo o

hard | if study | Japanese

oboemasu. / **If you study hard, you'll learn Japanese.**

will learn

Ano hito | ni aereba | shiawase desu. / **If I meet him, I'll be happy.**

him | if meet | will be happy

Yasumanakereba | byōki ni narimasu. / **Unless you rest you'll be sick.**

unless rest | sick | become

With verbal adjectives (-*i* adjectives), drop the -*i* and add *kereba*. For the negative, use the adverbial form (yasuku) [see **§8.2–3**] and add *nakereba*. For example:

Adjective	Conditional
yasui / **cheap**	yasukereba / **if it's cheap, if it were cheap**
	yasukunakereba / **if it's not cheap, unless it's cheap**

Examples

Yasukereba, | kaimasu. / **If it's cheap, I'll buy it.**

if cheap   buy

Samukereba, | kōto o kimasu. / **If it's cold, I'll put on an overcoat.**

if cold   coat   put on

Omoshirokereba, yomimasu. / **If it's interesting, I'll read it.**

if interesting   read

-tara form

The *-tara* form can express a wide range of conditional "when" and "if" meaning: past occurrence, hypothetical conditions in the past, future or habitual action. (See the forms below.)

To construct the *-tara* form, start with the plain past verb form and add *-ra*.

tabetara / **if I (you,** *etc.***) should eat (it)**

           if I (you, *etc.***) were to eat (it)**

           when I (you, *etc.***) eat (it)**

           when I (you, *etc.***) ate (it)**

For the negative, do the same: tabenakattara / **If I (you, etc.) didn't eat (it).**

Examples

Honya ni | ittara, | shimatte imashita. / **When I went to the bookstore, it was closed.**

bookstore when went   was closed

Benkyō shitara, | wakatta deshō. / **If I had studied, I would have understood.**

if had studied   understood

Kōhī o nondara, | neraremasen. / **When I drink coffee, I can't sleep.**

coffee when drink   can't sleep

Notice the use of *-tara* forms with *-i* and *-na* adjectives and with nouns.

Examples

Takakattara | kaimasen. / **If it's expensive, I won't buy it.**

if it is expensive won't buy

Soko ga | shizuka dattara | ikimasu. / **If it were quiet there, I would go.**

there   if it were quiet   would go

Ii hon | dattara, | kaimasu. / **If it were a good book, I would buy it.**

good   if it were   would buy

Other useful conditional forms are *nara* and *to*.

nara

with verbs	Present: iku nara / **if I (you, etc.) go** Past: itta nara / **if I had gone**
with verbal adjectives	Present: ōkii nara / **if it is / were big** Past: ōkikatta nara / **if it had been big**
with adjectival nouns	Present: kirei nara / **if it is / were pretty** Past: kirei datta nara / **if it had been pretty**
with nouns	gakusei nara / **if I am / were a student**

Similar to the *-tara* forms in meaning, *nara* can be used for **if** and **after**. In some uses, it has a strong contrary-to-fact element, like the subjunctive mood of English.

Examples

Watakushi ga kanemochi nara yotto o

rich person   if   sailboat

kaimasu.   / **If I were rich, I would buy a sailboat.**

would buy

Isogu nara, chikatetsu de ikinasai. / **If you're in a hurry,**
take a subway.

hurry   if   subway   take

to

To is used with the present forms of verbs and verbal adjectives, adjectival nouns, and with nouns. In many cases, the meaning is the same as that of the *-tara* or *-eba* forms.

Examples

Sake o nomu to, nemuku narimasu. / **Whenever I drink sake, I become sleepy.**

    drink **whenever** **sleepy** **become**

Tenki ga ii to, kōen ni ikimasu. / **When/if the weather is good, I go/ will go to the park.**

weather **good** **when/if** **park** **go**

§7.11 THE POTENTIAL MOOD

To express the idea of capability or possibility (**can** or **be able to** in English), add *-eru* (plain) or *-emasu* (polite) to the stem of c-stem verbs, and *-rareru* (plain) or *-raremasu* (polite) to the stem of v-stem verbs. The negatives are formed regularly: Add *-enai* / *-emasen* to the stem of c-stem verbs, and *-rarenai* / *-raremasen* to the stem of v-stem verbs.

Examples

Merī san wa, Nihongo ga hanasemasu. / **Mary can speak Japanese.**

    Japanese **can speak**

Nanji ni aemasu ka. / **What time can I see you?**

what time   can see

Kyō   ikenai nara, ashita | ikemasu | ka. / **If you
                                              can't go
                                              today, can
today can't go if tomorrow can go   ?   you go
                                              tomorrow?**

Another way to express the potential is as follows:

• Place the appropriate form of the verb *dekiru* / **can do** after
  a noun (plus the particle *ga*).

Examples

Nihongo ga dekimasu. / **I can speak Japanese.**

Japanese   can do

Tenisu ga dekimasu. / **I can play tennis.**

tennis   can do

Ryōri ga dekimasen. / **I can't cook.**

cooking   can't do

A verb form can be used with this structure as well, but it
must first be nominalized, or made into a noun form. To nomi-
nalize a verb, do the following:

- Add the word *koto* to the plain, or dictionary form, of the verb. Then it can be used with *ga* and *dekiru* / *dekimasu*.

Examples

Nihongo o yomu koto ga dekimasu. / **I can read Japanese.**

Japanese | read | can do

Merī san wa, oyogu koto ga dekimasen. / **Mary can't swim.**

swim | can't do

Kinō, Tanaka san ni au koto ga dekimashita.

yesterday | see | could do

/ **Yesterday, I could see Ms. Tanaka.**

§7.12 THE PASSIVE VOICE

Japanese has two ways of using the passive. The first is with transitive verbs, as in English. In such sentences, the "doer" may or may not be expressed. (**My wallet was stolen,** *or* **My wallet was stolen by a pickpocket.**)

- To form the passive, add *-areru*, *-aremasu* to the stems of c-stem verbs, and *-rareru*, *-raremasu* to the stems of v-stem verbs. For the negative, add *-arenai*, *-aremasen* to the stems of c-stem verbs, and *-rarenai*, *-raremasen* to the stems of v-stem verbs.

nusumu / **steal**, nusumareru, nusumaremasu / **is stolen**
oikakeru / **chase**, oikakerareru, oikakeraremasu / **is chased**

Examples

Kuruma ga nusumaremashita. / **My car was stolen.**

car   was stolen

Karate wa, Amerika de yoku | shirarete imasu. |

well   is known

/ **Karate is well-known in the United States.**

Sono hon wa kyonen kakaremashita. / **The book was written last year.**

book   last year   was written

Neko wa, inu   ni   oikakeraremashita. / **The cat was chased by a dog.**

cat   dog   by   was chased

So | mirarete imasu. | / **It is seen that way.**

that way   it is seen

- Note that the use of this type of passive is more limited in Japanese than in English. While passive forms are grammatically possible for many verbs, the resulting sentences may be awkward.

The second way of using the passive in Japanese, for which English has no corresponding use, may be called the "adversity" passive. You can think of it as the "too bad" or "regrettably" passive. This means that something happened to someone and it had an adverse effect on that person. The verb may be transitive or intransitive. Because this is quite unlike English, read the following sentences carefully, especially the translations.

- Note the use of *ni* in the passive sentences below.

  Examples

  Active
  Merī san no okāsan ga shinimashita. / **Mary's mother died.**

  Passive
  Merī san wa okāsan ni shinaremashita. / **Mary's mother died (on her). (Lit: Mary was died by her mother.)**

Active

Ame ga furimashita. / **It rained. (The rain fell.)**

rain   fell

Passive

Tanaka san wa ame ni furaremashita. / **Mr. Tanaka was caught in the rain. (Lit: Mr. Tanaka was fallen by rain.)**

rain by was fallen

§7.13 THE CAUSATIVE

The causative forms in Japanese express the idea of making or causing someone to do something: **I made my brother clean his room.** It also can mean **let** or **allow**: **Please let me go.**

- To form the causative, add *-aseru*, *-asemasu* to the stem of c-stem verbs (*-asenai*, *-asemasen* for the negative), and add *-saseru*, *-sasemasu* to the stem of v-stem verbs (*-sasenai*, *-sasemasen* for the negative).

yomu / **read**, yomaseru, yomasemasu / **make (someone) read let (someone) read**

taberu / **eat**, tabesaseru, tabesasemasu / **make (someone) eat let (someone) eat**

Examples

Merī san o mise ni ikasemashita. / **I made Mary go to the store.**

store to made go

Okāsan wa, kodomo o nekasemashita. / **The mother made the child go to bed.**

mother child made sleep

Watakushi ni harawasete kudasai. / **Please let me pay.**

let pay please

Otōto ni | benkyō sasemashita. | / **I made my younger brother study.**

younger brother made study

§7.14 THE CAUSATIVE PASSIVE

The causative passive form expresses the idea that the subject of the sentence is made to do something in the sense of being forced.

• To form the causative passive, add *-aserareru*, *-aseraremasu* to the stem of c-stem verbs (*-aserarenai*, *-aseraremasen* for the negative), and add *-saserareru*, *-saseraremasu* to the stem of v-stem verbs (*-saserarenai*, *-saseraremasen* for the negative).

iku / **go**	ikaserareru, ikaseraremasu / **be made to go**
taberu / **eat**	tabesaserareru, tabesaseraremasu / **be made to eat**

Examples

Kyōkasho o | kawaseraremashita. | / **I was made to buy a textbook.**

textbook **was made to buy**

Kodomo wa, miruku o nomaseraremashita. / **The child was made to drink (his) milk.**

child **milk** **was made to drink**

Jon san wa, | asa gohan | o | tsukuraseraremashita. |

breakfast **was forced to make**
/ **John was forced to make breakfast.**

§7.15 THE GIVING AND RECEIVING VERBS

Japanese has several verbs for conveying the meaning of *giving* and *receiving*. Choosing which one to use involves the relative status of the giver and receiver. It also involves the direction of the action, in the sense of giving *to* and receiving *from*.

- The following verbs are used to describe someone's giving something to you, the speaker, or to someone in your in-group, as in the diagram below the box.

To say, **Give kindly (to me** or **my in-group: family, friends, etc.)**, use:
kureru
kudasaru (use for referring to superiors)

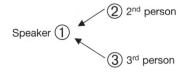

Speaker ①
② 2ⁿᵈ person
③ 3ʳᵈ person

Examples

Haha ga watakushi ni kuremashita. / **My mother gave it to me.**

| | | | |
my mother   me   to   gave

Kore wa tomodachi ga kureta hon desu. / **This is the book my friend gave me.**

| | | | |
this   friend   gave book is

Sensei ga jisho o kudasaimashita. / **The teacher gave me a dictionary.**

| | |
teacher dictionary   gave

• The following verbs are used for **I give**, **he gives**, etc., as in the diagram below the box.

> To say **give**, use:
> *ageru*
> *sashiageru* (use for speaking to or referring to superiors)

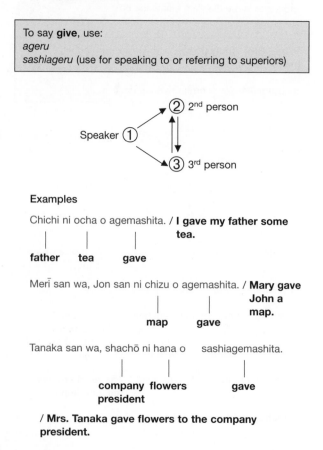

Examples

Chichi ni ocha o agemashita. / **I gave my father some tea.**

| | | |
| father | tea | gave |

Merī san wa, Jon san ni chizu o agemashita. / **Mary gave John a map.**

| | |
| map | gave |

Tanaka san wa, shachō ni hana o   sashiagemashita.

| | | |
| company president | flowers | gave |

/ **Mrs. Tanaka gave flowers to the company president.**

- The following verbs are used for **receive**, as in the diagram below the box.

> To say **receive**, use:
> *morau*
> *itadaku* (use for speaking to or referring to superiors)

Examples

Jon san wa, tomodachi   ni shīdī o moraimashita.

	friend	**from CD**	**received**

/ **John received a CD from his friend.**

Chichi wa, kaisha   kara   bōnasu o   moraimashita.

father	**company**	**from**	**bonus**	**received**

/ **Father received a bonus from the company.**

Sensei   kara tegami o itadakimashita. / **I got a letter from the teacher.**

teacher	**from**	**letter**	**got**

The giving and receiving verbs are often used as auxiliaries after the gerund, or -*te* form of another verb. In this usage, the relationship between the giver and the receiver is as described in the verbs given above. When speaking to or about a superior, be sure to use the appropriate verb.

- Keep in mind that these forms can mean not just giving or receiving something tangible, but also giving or receiving the action or sense of the verb.

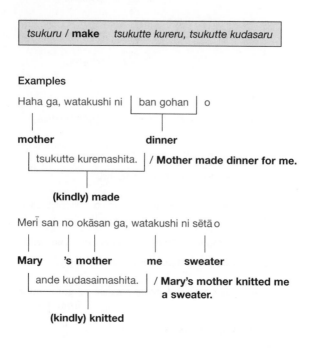

tsukuru / **make**   *tsukutte kureru, tsukutte kudasaru*

Examples

Haha ga, watakushi ni │ ban gohan │ o

mother   **dinner**

│ tsukutte kuremashita. │ / **Mother made dinner for me.**

(kindly) made

Merī san no okāsan ga, watakushi ni sētā o

Mary   **'s mother**   **me**   **sweater**

│ ande kudasaimashita. │ / **Mary's mother knitted me a sweater.**

(kindly) knitted

kau / **buy**   *katte ageru, katte sashiageru*

Examples

Tanaka san ga, Jon san ni sore o

|
it

| katte agemashita. | / **Mr. Tanaka bought it for John.**

bought

Suzuki san wa, shachō ni nekutai o

| |
company   **necktie**
president

| katte sashiagemashita. | / **Mr. Suzuki bought the company president a tie.**

bought

iku / **go** *itte morau, itte itadaku*

Examples

Ane ni kaimono ni | itte moraimashita. | / **I had my elder sister go shopping for me.**

| |
elder shopping   **had go**
sister

Honda san ni yūbinkyoku e | itte itadakimashita. |

post office   **had go**

/ **I had Mr. Honda go to the post office for me.**

§7.16 THE HONORIFIC AND HUMBLE FORMS

Using the correct language to reflect relationships is important to the Japanese. This means expressing the appropriate degree of respect or deference to the listener, and the appropriate degree of humility about oneself or one's family. The speaker's attitude toward the listener or the person being spoken about is the key. Honorific language elevates someone else; humble language lowers oneself.

| Tip | Using the honorific and humble verb forms confidently takes a good deal of experience with Japanese culture, but the forms themselves are not difficult to learn. |

The honorifics of verbs take several forms.

• One honorific form is the passive form itself (see **§7.12**).

Plain Form	Passive and Honorific Form
aruku / **walk**	arukareru
kaeru / **change**	kaerareru
suru / **do**	sareru
kuru / **come**	korareru

- Another set of honorific forms can be made as follows:

> *o* + infinitive + *desu*

---

yobu / **call**   *oyobi desu (honorific form)*

Examples

Shachō ga | oyobi desu. | / **The company president is**
                          calling you.

company   **is calling**
president

Shachō ga oyobi deshita. / **The company president was**
                              calling you.

> *o* + infinitive + *ni naru*

Examples

Shachō ga | oyobi ni narimashita. | / **The company**
                                     president called
                                     you.

                called

Hon o | oyomi ni narimashita | ka. / **Have you read this**
                                     book?

book   **read**

o + infinitive + *kudasai* / **Please (do it).**

Examples

Tanaka san o │ oyobi kudasai. │ / **Please call Mr. Tanaka.**

please call

Shōshō │ omachi kudasai. │ / **Please wait a moment.**

a little   **please wait**

• The humble forms can be constructed as follows:

o + infinitive + *suru*

Examples

Watakushi ga Tanaka san o │ oyobi shimasu. │ / **I'll call Mr. Tanaka.**

will call

Hiru made ni │ onaoshi shimasu. │ / **I'll fix it by noon.**

noon   **by**   **will fix**

o + infinitive + *itasu*

Examples

Sugu │ omochi itashimasu. │ / **I'll bring it immediately.**

immediately will bring

Kasa o | okashi itashimashō ka. | / **Shall I lend you an umbrella?**

umbrella   **shall lend**

- Some verbs have special honorific and humble forms. Following are a few commonly used examples.

Verb	Honorific	Humble
iku / **go**	irassharu	mairu
kuru / **come**	irassharu	mairu
iru / **be**	irassharu	oru
suru / **do**	nasaru	itasu
iu / **say**	ossharu	mōsu
taberu / **eat**	meshiagaru	itadaku
miru / **see**	goran ni naru	haiken suru

§7.17 CLAUSES

Dependent Clauses

Unlike English, independent clauses in Japanese cannot be strung together in one sentence and joined by a conjunction like "and." In Japanese, the main or independent clause comes at the *end* of the sentence, and other clauses are *dependent*. Following are some basic ways in which dependent clauses are linked to the main, or independent clause.

... *-te/de*

- The *-te* or gerund form of the verb can be used to indicate sequential, parallel, or causal relationships of dependent clauses. Verbal adjectives (the *-kute* form) and adjectival nouns (with the *de* form of the copula) can also be used this way (See **§8**), as can nouns (with the *de* form of the copula). Look at the examples.

Sequential:	As the name implies, this form is used for actions that occur in a time sequence: **first, then, then,** etc.

Example

Ginza e itte   kaimono o shite, uchi e   kaerimashita.

went	**shopping**	**did**	**home**	**returned**

/ **I went to Ginza, did some shopping, and returned home.**

Parallel:	The action or meaning here is parallel, or can take place at the same time.

Examples

Yamada san wa Ginza e itte, watakushi wa Shinjuku e

                |

              went

ikimashita. / **Mrs. Yamada went to Ginza, and I went**
  | **to Shinjuku.**

  went

Kono heya wa, hirokute   akarukute rippa desu.
 | | | | | |
this room   is spacious is bright gorgeous is

/ **This room is spacious and bright and gorgeous.**

 Causal: The dependent clause shows the cause, the main clause shows the effect. The cause-effect relationship need not be a strong one, however, for the *-te* form to be used.

Examples

Sensō ga owatte | ureshii desu. | / **I'm glad because the war is over.**

  | | |

war is over am glad

Yamada san wa, byōki de | kimasen. | / **Ms. Yamada isn't coming because she's sick.**

         | | |

sick is isn't coming

Kono heya wa akarukute | kimochi ga ii desu. / **I feel good because this room is bright.**

this room   is bright   feeling is good

> . . . -tari . . . -tari

- This form is used for **do things like . . .** or **sometimes this, sometimes that**.

  Examples

  Shūmatsu wa, nani o shimasu ka. / **What do you do on weekends?**

  weekends   what   do

  Eiga o mitari, tenisu o shitari shimasu. / **I do things like seeing a movie and/or playing tennis.**

  movie like seeing   tennis   like playing   do

  Haha   no   ryōri wa, oishikattari mazukattari shimasu.

  mother's   cooking   sometimes good   sometimes bad   does

  / **My mother's cooking is sometimes good, sometimes bad.**

> ... -*shi* ... -*shi*

- This form is used for **and in addition, and what's more.**

Examples

Kono shūmatsu wa iroiro shimashita. / **I did various things this weekend.**

Kaimono o shita shi, kuruma o aratta shi, Nihongo mo benkyō shimashita. / **I went shopping, washed my car, and studied Japanese.**

shopping	did and	car		washed and			
		studied					

Kono shūmatsu wa, totemo taihen deshita. / **This weekend was awful (very bad).**

this	weekend	very	bad	was	

Kuruma o nusumareta shi, saifu o nakushita shi,

car	was stolen	and	wallet	lost	and what's more

inu ni kamaremashita. / **My car was stolen, I lost my wallet, and what's more, I was bitten by a dog.**

dog	by	was bitten

Relative Clauses

Japanese does not have relative pronouns like the English
who, **that**, **which**, for use in relative clauses such as **The
man who arrived is my friend**. Instead, the relative
clause, ending with the plain form of the verb, comes
before the word it modifies.

Examples

Watakushi ga/no itsumo iku restoran wa, Ginza

| | | | |
| I | always | go | restaurant |

ni arimasu. / **The restaurant that I always go to is
in Ginza.**

in   is

Kondo no ryokō de itta tokoro wa, Amerika to

this   trip   went   places
time

Kanada   deshita. / **The places that I went to on this
trip were America and Canada.**

Canada   were

§7.18 COMMON EXPRESSIONS WITH VERBS AND ADJECTIVES

The following forms are useful, some with verbs, some with both verbs and adjectives. If you use the *-de*, *demo*, or *dewa* forms, they can be used with nouns or adjectival nouns as well.

| *-temo ii desu* / | It's okay if . . . |
| | You may . . . |

Examples

Takakutemo | ii desu. / **It's okay (even) if it's expensive.**

if expensive   is okay

Tabetemo | ii desu. / **You may eat.**

if eat   is okay

| *-nakutemo ii desu* / | It's okay even if it's not . . . |
| | You don't have to . . . |

Examples

Yasukunakutemo | ii desu. / **It's okay even if it's not cheap.**

even if not cheap   is okay

Tabenakutemo | ii desu. / **You don't have to eat.**

if don't eat   is okay

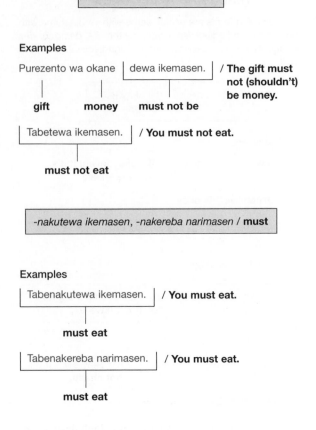

| *-tewa ikemasen* / **must not** |

Examples

Purezento wa okane | dewa ikemasen. | / **The gift must not (shouldn't) be money.**

gift   money   must not be

Tabetewa ikemasen. | / **You must not eat.**

must not eat

| *-nakutewa ikemasen, -nakereba narimasen* / **must** |

Examples

Tabenakutewa ikemasen. | / **You must eat.**

must eat

Tabenakereba narimasen. | / **You must eat.**

must eat

beki desu / **should** (obligation), **ought to**

Examples

Motto | benkyō suru | beki desu. / **You should study more.**

more   study   should

Motto ganbaru | beki desu. / **You should try harder.**

more try hard   should

hazu desu / **is expected** (no moral obligation), supposition

Examples

Mada | nete iru | hazu desu. / **He should still be sleeping.**

still   is sleeping   should

Kotoshi no natsu   Nihon   e   iku

this year's summer   go

hazu deshita. / **I was supposed to go to Japan this summer.**

was supposed to

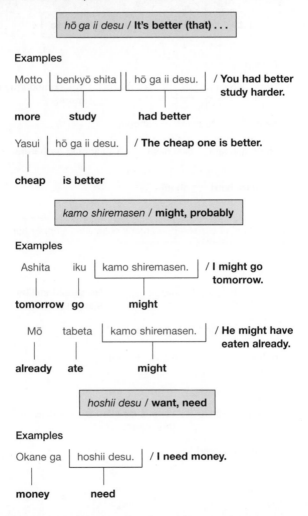

| *hō ga ii desu* / **It's better (that) . . .** |

Examples

Motto | benkyō shita | hō ga ii desu. | / **You had better study harder.**
more | study | had better

Yasui | hō ga ii desu. | / **The cheap one is better.**
cheap | is better

| *kamo shiremasen* / **might, probably** |

Examples

Ashita | iku | kamo shiremasen. | / **I might go tomorrow.**
tomorrow | go | might

Mō | tabeta | kamo shiremasen. | / **He might have eaten already**
already | ate | might

| *hoshii desu* / **want, need** |

Examples

Okane ga | hoshii desu. | / **I need money.**
money | need

Kōhī ga | hoshikatta desu. | / **I wanted coffee.**

coffee   wanted

-*tai desu* / **want**

Examples

Sushi ga | tabetai desu. | / **I want to eat sushi.**

want to eat

Sakana wa | tabetaku arimasen. | / **I don't want to eat fish.**

fish   don't want to eat

§7.19 NOMINALIZATION

Verbs or clauses can be nominalized, or made into nouns, by using *no* or *koto* immediately after. Note that *koto* is more formal and can be used in the predicate; *no* is less formal and cannot be used in the predicate (see **§3.3–2**).

Examples

Watakushi wa | taberu no | ga daisuki desu. / **I like eating very much.**

eating

Ryokō suru no | wa | tanoshii | desu. / **I enjoy traveling.**

traveling — enjoyable

Anata ga itta koto | wa | tadashii desu. / **What you said was right.**

What you said — was right

Miru koto | wa | shinjiru koto | desu. / **Seeing is believing.**

Seeing — believing

Suru yori iu no | wa | kantan | desu. / **It's easier said than done.**

Saying than doing — easy

Yamada san wa | oshieru no | o yamemashita. / **Mr. Yamada quit teaching.**

teaching — quit

§7.20 VERB CHARTS

In the following charts you will find conjugated forms of a sample of Japanese verbs.

aru / **to exist, to be (inanimate)**

Stem: ar-   Intransitive

		Affirmative	Negative
Present:	Plain	aru	nai
	Polite	arimasu	arimasen
Past	Plain	atta	nakatta
	Polite	arimashita	arimasen deshita
Gerund (-*te* form):		atte	nakute
Presumptive:	Plain	aru darō	nai darō
	Polite	aru deshō	nai deshō
Imperative:	Plain		
	Polite		
Conditional:	Plain	areba	nakereba
		attara	nakattara
		aru to	nai to
		aru nara	nai nara

Plain Affirmative

Potential:		Polite*	gozaru
Passive:			
Causative:			
Causative Passive:		Humble:	

*Because the subject is inanimate, this is neither honorific nor humble; it is neutral polite.

da / **to be, to equal**

Stem:			Intransitive
		Affirmative	Negative
Present:	Plain	da	dewa nai ja nai
	Polite	desu	dewa arimasen ja arimasen
Past	Plain	datta	dewa nakatta ja nakatta

	Polite	deshita	dewa arimasen
			   deshita
			ja arimasen
			   deshita

Gerund (-te form):		de	dewa nakutte ja nakute
Presumptive:	Plain	darō	dewa nai darō ja nai darō
		deshō	dewa nai deshō ja nai deshō
Imperative:	Plain		
	Polite		
Conditional:	Plain	dattara	dewa nakattara ja nakattara
		da to	dewa nai to ja nai to
		nara	ja nai nara ja nakereba

	Plain Affirmative	
Potential:		Honorific:
Passive:		
Causative:		
Causative		Humble:
Passive:		

hanasu / **to speak**

Stem: hanas-			Transitive
		Affirmative	Negative
Present:	Plain	hanasu	hanasanai
	Polite	hanashimasu	hanashimasen
Past:	Plain	hanashita	hanasanakatta
	Polite	hanashimashita	hanashimasen deshita
Gerund (-*te* form):		hanashite	hanasanaide hanasanakute
Presumptive:	Plain	hanasu darō	hanasanai darō
	Polite	hanasu deshō	hanasanai deshō
	Plain	hanasō	hanasumai
	Polite	hanashimashō	
Imperative:	Plain	hanase	hanasuna
	Polite	hanashinasai	
		hanashite kudasai	hanasanaide kudasai
Conditional:		hanaseba	hanasanakereba
		hanashitara	hanasanakattara
		hanasu to	hanasanai to

Plain Affirmative

Potential:	hanaseru	Honorific:	ohanashi ni naru
Passive:	hanasareru		hanasareru
Causative:	hanasaseru	Humble:	ohanashi suru
			ohanashi itasu
Causative Passive:	hanasaserareru		

iku / **to go**

Stem: ik-			Intransitive

		Affirmative	Negative
Present:	Plain	iku	ikanai
	Polite	ikimasu	ikimasen
Past:	Plain	itta	ikanakatta
	Polite	ikimashita	ikimasen deshita
Gerund (-*te* form):		itte	ikanaide ikanakute
Presumptive:	Plain	iku darō	ikanai darō
	Polite	iku deshō	ikanai deshō
	Plain	ikō	ikumai
	Polite	ikimashō	
Imperative:	Plain	ike	ikuna
	Polite	ikinasai	
		itte kudasai	ikanaide kudasai
Conditional:		ikeba	ikanakereba
		ittara	ikanakattara
		iku to	ikanai to
		iku nara	ikanai nara

Plain Affirmative

Potential:	ikeru	Honorific:	irassharu
Passive:	ikareru		
Causative:	ikaseru	Humble:	mairu
Causative Passive:	ikaserareru		

iru / **to exist, to be (animate)**

Stem: i-   Intransitive

		Affirmative	Negative
Present:	Plain	iru	inai
	Polite	imasu	imasen
Past	Plain	ita	inakatta
	Polite	imashita	imasen deshita
Gerund (-*te* form):		ite	inai de
			inakute
Presumptive:	Plain	iru darō	inai darō
	Polite	iru deshō	inai deshō
	Plain	iyō	
	Polite	imashō	
Imperative:	Plain	iro	iruna
	Polite	inasai	
		ite kudasai	inai de kudasai
Conditional:	Plain	ireba	inakereba
		itara	inakattara
		iru to	inai to
		iru nara	inai nara

Plain Affirmative

Potential:	irareru	Honorific:	irassharu
			oide ni naru
			irareru
Passive:	irareru		
Causative:	isaseru		
Causative Passive:	isaserareru	Humble:	oru

kaeru / **to return**

Stem: kaer-			Intransitive
		Affirmative	Negative
Present:	Plain	kaeru	kaeranai
	Polite	kaerimasu	kaerimasen
Past:	Plain	kaetta	kaeranakatta
	Polite	kaerimashita	kaerimasen deshita
Gerund (-*te* form):		kaette	kaeranaide kaeranakute
Presumptive:	Plain	kaeru darō	kaeranai darō
	Polite	kaeru deshō	kaeranai deshō
	Plain	kaerō	kaerumai
	Polite	kaerimashō	
Imperative:	Plain	kaere	kaeruna
	Polite	karinasai	
		kaette kudasai	kaeranaide kudasai
Conditional:		kaereba	kaeranakereba
		kaettara	kaeranakattara
		kaeru to	kaeranai to

Plain Affirmative

Potential:	kaereru	Honorific:	okaeri ni naru
Passive:	kaerareru		kaerareru
Causative:	kaeraseru	Humble:	————
Causative Passive:	kaeraserareru kaerasareru		

kau / **to buy**

Stem: ka-			Transitive
		Affirmative	Negative
Present:	Plain	kau	kawanai
	Polite	kaimasu	kaimasen
Past:	Plain	katta	kawanakatta
	Polite	kaimashita	kaimasen deshita
Gerund (-*te* form):		katte	kawanaide kawanakute
Presumptive:	Plain	kau darō	kawanai darō
	Polite	kau deshō	kawanai deshō
	Plain	kaō	kaumai
	Polite	kaimashō	
Imperative:	Plain	kae	kauna
	Polite	kainasai	
		katte kudasai	kawanaide kudasai
Conditional:		kaeba	kawanakereba
		kattara	kawanakattara
		kau to	kawanai to
		kau nara	kawanai nara

Plain Affirmative

Potential:	kaeru	Honorific:	okai ni naru
Passive:	kawareru		kawareru
Causative:	kawaseru		
Causative Passive:	kawaserareru kawasareru		

kiku / **to listen, to ask, to hear**

Stem: kik-			Transitive
		Affirmative	Negative
Present:	Plain	kiku	kikanai
	Polite	kikimasu	kikimasen
Past:	Plain	kiita	kikanakatta
	Polite	kikimashita	kikimasen deshita
Gerund (-*te* form):		kiite	kikanaide kikanakute
Presumptive:	Plain	kiku darō	kikanai darō
	Polite	kiku deshō	kikanai deshō
	Plain	kikō	kikumai
	Polite	kikimashō	
Imperative:	Plain	kike	kikuna
	Polite	kikinasai	
		kiite kudasai	kikanaide kudasai
Conditional:		kikeba	kikanakereba
		kiitara	kikanakattara
		kiku to	kikanai to
		kiku nara	kikanai nara

Plain Affirmative

Potential:	kikeru	Honorific:	okiki ni naru
Passive:	kikareru		kikareru
Causative:	kikaseru	Humble:	ukagau (to ask)
Causative Passive:	kikaserareru		okiki suru (to ask)
	kikasareru		

kuru / **to come**

Stem: ku-			Intransitive
		Affirmative	Negative
Present:	Plain	kuru	konai
	Polite	kimasu	kimasen
Past:	Plain	kita	konakatta
	Polite	kimashita	kimasen deshita
Gerund (-*te* form):		kite	konaide konakute
Presumptive:	Plain	kuru darō	konai darō
	Polite	kuru deshō	konai deshō
	Plain	koyō	kurumai
	Polite	kimashō	
Imperative:	Plain	koi	kuruna
	Polite	kinasai	
		kite kudasai	konaide kudasai
Conditional:		kureba	konakereba
		kitara	konakattara
		kuru to	konai to
		kuru nara	konai nara

Plain Affirmative

Potential:	korareru	Honorific:	irassharu
Passive:	korareru		oide ni naru korareru
Causative:	kosaseru	Humble:	mairu
Causative Passive:	kosaserareru		

miru / **to look at, to see**

Stem: mi-			Transitive
		Affirmative	Negative
Present:	Plain	miru	minai
	Polite	mimasu	mimasen
Past:	Plain	mita	minakatta
	Polite	mimashita	mimasen deshita
Gerund (-*te* form):		mite	minaide
			minakute
Presumptive:	Plain	miru darō	minai darō
	Polite	miru deshō	minai deshō
	Plain	miyō	mimai
	Polite	mimashō	
Imperative:	Plain	miro	miruna
	Polite	minasai	
		mite kudasai	minaide kudasai
Conditional:		mireba	minakereba
		mitara	minakattara
		miru to	minai to
		miru nara	minai nara

Plain Affirmative

Potential:	mirareru	Honorific:	goran ni naru
Passive:	mirareru		mirareru
Causative:	misaseru	Humble:	haiken suru
Causative Passive:	misaserareru		haiken itasu

nomu / **to drink**

Stem: nom-			Transitive
		Affirmative	Negative
Present:	Plain	nomu	nomanai
	Polite	nomimasu	nomimasen
Past:	Plain	nonda	nomanakatta
	Polite	nomimashita	nomimasen deshita
Gerund (-*te* form):		nonde	nomanaide nomanakute
Presumptive:	Plain	nomu darō	nomanai darō
	Polite	nomu deshō	nomanai deshō
	Plain	nomō	nomumai
	Polite	nomimashō	
Imperative:	Plain	nome	nomuna
	Polite	nomimasai	
		nonde kudasai	nomanaide kudasai
Conditional:		nomeba	nomanakereba
		nondara	nomanakattara
		nomu to	nomanai to
		nomu nara	nomanai nara

Plain Affirmative

Potential:	nomeru	Honorific:	onomi ni naru
Passive:	nomareru		nomareru
Causative:	nomaseru	Humble:	itadaku
Causative Passive:	nomaserareru nomasareru		

suru / to do, to make

Stem: su-			Transitive
		Affirmative	Negative
Present:	Plain	suru	shinai
	Polite	shimasu	shimasen
Past:	Plain	shita	shinakatta
	Polite	shimashita	shimasen deshita
Gerund (-*te* form):		shite	shinaide shinakute
Presumptive:	Plain	suru darō	shinai darō
	Polite	suru deshō	shinai deshō
	Plain	shiyō	surumai
	Polite	shimashō	
Imperative:	Plain	shiro	suruna
	Polite	shinasai	
		shite kudasai	shinaide kudasai
Conditional:		sureba	shinakereba
		shitara	shinakattara
		suru to	shinai to
		suru nara	shinai nara

Plain Affirmative

Potential:	dekiru	Honorific:	nasaru
Passive:	sareru		sareru
Causative:	saseru	Humble:	itasu
Causative Passive:	saserareru		

taberu / **to eat**

Stem: tabe-			Transitive
		Affirmative	Negative
Present:	Plain	taberu	tabenai
	Polite	tabemasu	tabemasen
Past:	Plain	tabeta	tabenakatta
	Polite	tabemashita	tabemasen deshita
Gerund (-*te* form):		tabete	tabenaide tabenakute
Presumptive:	Plain	taberu darō	tabenai darō
	Polite	taberu deshō	tabenai deshō
	Plain	tabeyō	tabemai
	Polite	tabemashō	
Imperative:	Plain	tabero tabenasai	taberuna
	Polite	tabete kudasai	tabenaide kudasai
Conditional:		tabereba tabetara taberu to taberu nara	tabenakereba tabenakattara tabenai to tabenai nara

Plain Affirmative

Potential:	taberareru	Honorific:	meshiagaru
Passive:	taberareru		otabe ni naru
Causative:	tabesaseru		taberareru
Causative Passive:	tabesaserareru	Humble:	itadaku

wakaru / **to understand**

Stem: wakar-   Intransitive

		Affirmative	Negative
Present:	Plain	wakaru	wakaranai
	Polite	wakarimasu	wakarimasen
Past:	Plain	wakatta	wakaranakatta
	Polite	wakarimashita	wakarimasen deshita
Gerund (-*te* form):		wakatte	wakaranaide wakaranakute
Presumptive:	Plain	wakaru darō	wakaranai darō
	Polite	wakaru deshō	wakaranai deshō
	Plain	wakarō	wakarumai
	Polite		
Imperative:	Plain	wakare	
	Polite	wakatte kudasai	
Conditional:		wakareba	wakaranakereba
		wakattara	wakaranakattara
		wakaru to	wakaranai to
		wakaru nara	wakaranai nara

Plain Affirmative

Potential:	———————	Honorific:	owakari ni naru
Passive:	———————		
Causative:	wakaraseru	Humble:	———————
Causative Passive:	wakaraserareru		

§8.

Adjectives

§8.1 WHAT ARE ADJECTIVES?

English speakers define *adjectives* as "words which modify or describe nouns."

The Japanese adjective, however, does not fit neatly into the definition of the English adjective. Therefore, speakers of English must be prepared for new ways of looking at adjectives, which in Japanese are quite unlike their English counterparts.

What are the major differences? To put it simply, Japanese adjectives fall into two groups: one group has verb-like characteristics, and the other group has noun-like characteristics. Both groups may function like English adjectives, that is, to modify nouns that follow. With this concept in mind, Japanese adjectives can be understood easily.

One group may be called *verbal adjectives*, the other *adjectival nouns*. We shall look at each group separately. First, the verbal adjectives.

§8.2 VERBAL ADJECTIVES

Adjectives in this group, in their dictionary form, end only in *-ai*, *-ii* , *-oi*, or *-ui*. Thus, they are often referred to as *-i* adjectives.

Here are some common -*i* adjectives.

-*i* Adjectives	
chiisai / **small**	takai / **expensive**
yasui / **inexpensive, cheap**	ōkii / **big**
oishii / **delicious**	ii / **good, nice**
yasashii / **easy**	warui / **bad**
atarashii / **new** **difficult**	muzukashii /
omoshiroi / **interesting**	amai / **sweet**
suzushii / **cool**	wakai / **young**
hayai / **fast, early**	itai / **painful**
kuroi / **black**	shiroi / **white**

§8.2–1 Noun Modifiers

The -*i* adjective in the forms listed above can modify a noun that follows, just as an English adjective does:

Examples

chiisai kuruma / **small car**

kuroi kutsu / **black shoes**

omoshiroi hon / **interesting book**

ii hito / **good person**

Atarashii kuruma o | kaimasu. | / **I will buy a new car.**

new   car   will buy

Oishii kudamono o tabemashita. / **We ate some delicious fruit.**

fruit

§8.2–2 Verbal Forms

The forms given in **§8.2** are the dictionary form of the verbal adjectives. As verbal forms, they have the characteristics of verbs, as you will see below.

> They have stems.

To form the stem, drop the final -*i*. This is the form used to make all the other forms of the adjective.

-i Adjective	Stem
akai / **red**	aka-
omoshiroi / **interesting**	omoshiro-
nagai / **long**	naga-
yasui / **cheap**	yasu-

> As is, they form the predicate.

Tip

Since the dictionary form is the plain present form of the verb, you can think of the verbal adjective as already containing in itself the grammatical form of the copula, or **is**. And, since a Japanese sentence requires a predicate but not a subject if the context is clear, each verbal adjective can constitute a sentence. There can, of course, be other elements in the sentence.

Note that these are plain forms.

Examples

Suzushii. / **It's cool.**

Muzukashii. / **It's difficult.**

Atama ga itai. / **My head hurts.**

Kono hon wa, omoshiroi. / **This book is interesting.**

> They conjugate, or change form, for different tenses and moods.

- To form the plain past tense, add -*katta* to the stem.

Plain	
Present	**Past**
suzushii / **is cool**	suzushikatta / **was cool**
oishii / **is delicious**	oishikatta / **was delicious**
chiisai / **is small**	chiisakatta / **was small**
wakai / **is young**	wakakatta / **was young**
osoi / **is slow**	osokatta / **was slow**

- To form the negative of the plain present and past, add -*ku* to the stem. Then, as with regular plain past verbs, add the appropriate form of *nai*.

Plain Negative	
Present	**Past**
suzushiku nai / **isn't cool**	suzushikunakatta / **wasn't cool**
chiisaku nai / **isn't small**	chiisakunakatta / **wasn't small**

- For the polite forms, add *desu* to the plain form for the present and the past.

Polite	
Present	**Past**
suzushii desu / **is cool**	suzushikatta desu / **was cool**
chiisai desu / **is small**	chiisakatta desu / **was small**

- To form the polite negative, use the *-ku* form, and add *arimasen* to the present, and *arimasen deshita* to the past.

Polite Negative	
Present	**Past**
suzushiku arimasen / **isn't cool**	suzushiku arimasen deshita / **wasn't cool**
chiisaku arimasen / **isn't small**	chiisaku arimasen deshita / **wasn't small**

- A variation of the polite negative forms may be formed by adding *desu* to the plain negative forms:

suzushiiku nai desu / **isn't cool**	suzushikunakatta desu / **wasn't cool**
chiisaku nai desu / **isn't small**	chiisakunakatta desu / **wasn't small**

- To form the gerund, add *-kute* to the stem.

  Example

  Kono hon wa omoshirokute | tanoshii desu. | / **This book is interesting and enjoyable.**

  book is interesting   **is enjoyable**

- For other verb moods, the verbal adjective forms can be expanded as follows:

  Presumptive: atsui deshō / **will probably be hot**

  Conditional: atsukereba / **if it were hot**

  atsukunakereba / **if it were not hot**

  atsukutemo / **even if it's hot**

  and so forth (see **§7** and **§8.2–4**).

The following examples illustrate some uses of the verbal adjective forms presented in this section.

Examples

Kono kutsu wa, | chiisai desu. | / **These shoes are small.**

shoes   are small

Ano hon wa, | yasukatta desu. | / **That book was cheap.**

was cheap

Hiru gohan wa, | oishikatta desu. | / **Lunch was delicious.**

lunch   was delicious

Shiken wa | yasashikatta desu. | / **The exam was easy.**

exam   was easy

Kono kuruma wa, | atarashiku nai desu. | / **This car isn't new.**

car   isn't new

Sono eiga wa, | omoshiroku arimasen deshita. | / **That movie wasn't interesting.**

movie   **wasn't interesting**

Heya wa, | suzushikunakatta desu. | / **The room wasn't cool.**

room   **wasn't cool**

§8.2–3 Adverbial Forms

To form adverbs from the -*i* adjectives, just add -*ku* to the stem. Or, to put it another way, change the final -*i* to -*ku*.

Adjective	Adverb
omoshiroi / **interesting**	omoshiroku / **interesting**
hayai / **quick**	hayaku / **quick, quickly**
warui / **bad**	waruku / **bad, badly**
ii / **good**	yoku* / **well**
takai / **expensive**	takaku / **expensive**
kuroi / **black**	kuroku / **black**

*This is an irregular form.

Note how the adverbs are used in sentences. Look at the kinds of verbs typically used with adverbs, especially *naru*, **become**.

Examples

Shōsetsu ga, omoshiroku narimashita. / **The novel became interesting.**
or
I have become interested in novels.

novel	interesting	became

Hayaku ikinasai. / **Go quickly.**

quickly	go

Hayaku arukimashita. / **I walked quickly.**

Tenki ga waruku narimashita. / **The weather became bad.**

weather	bad	became

Tarō san wa, yoku benkyō shimashita. / **Taro studied well.**

well	studied

Yachin ga takaku narimashita. / **The rent became expensive.**

rent	expensive	became

Doa o kuroku nurimashita. / **I painted the door black.**

door	black	painted

Ano hito wa, eigo ga yoku wakarimasu. / **He understands
English well.**

| | | |
| | | |

English   well understands

Yoku nemashita. / **I slept well.**

| | |
| | |

well   slept

§8.2–4   VERBAL ADJECTIVE CHARTS

In the following charts you will find conjugated forms of a
sample of verbal adjectives.

itai / **painful**

Stem: ita-		Verbal Adjective	
		Affirmative	Negative
Present:	Plain	itai	itaku nai
	Polite	itai desu	itaku arimasen
Past:	Plain	itakatta	itakunakatta
	Polite	itakatta desu	itakunakatta desu
			itaku arimasen deshita
Gerund (-*te* form):		itakute	itakunakute
Presumptive:	Plain	itai darō	itaku nai darō
	Polite	itai deshō	itaku nai deshō
Conditional:		itakereba	itaku nakereba
		itakattara	itaku nakattara
		itai to	itakunai to
		itai nara	itakunai nara

ōkii / **big**

Stem: ōki-		Verbal Adjective	
		Affirmative	Negative
Present:	Plain	ōkii	ōkiku nai
	Polite	ōkii desu	ōkiku arimasen
Past:	Plain	ōkikatta	ōkikunakatta
	Polite	ōkikatta desu	ōkikunakatta desu
			ōkiku arimasen deshita
Gerund (-*te* form):		ōkikute	ōkikunakute
Presumptive:	Plain	ōkii darō	ōkiku nai darō
	Polite	ōkii deshō	ōkiku nai deshō
Conditional:		ōkikereba	ōkiku nakereba
		ōkikattara	ōkiku nakattara
		ōkii to	ōkikunai to
		ōkii nara	okikunai nara

§8.3 ADJECTIVAL NOUNS

Words in this group have noun-like characteristics and can convey adjectival meanings. When they modify nouns, they are followed by the suffix *-na*. Thus, they are often referred to as *-na* adjectives.

Here are some common *-na* adjectives.

-na **Adjectives**	
shizuka / **quiet**	kirei / **pretty**
genki / **well, healthy**	benri / **convenient**
shinsetsu / **kind**	yūmei / **famous**
jōzu / **good at**	heta / **not good at**
dame / **no good**	suki / **like**
fuben / **inconvenient**	iroiro / **various**
shōjiki / **honest**	teinei / **polite**

Tip

You may notice that these words, as translated, do not fit neatly into the English notion of adjectives. The following sections should help clarify their usage.

§8.3–1 Noun Modifiers

With the addition of *-na*, the words in the preceding chart can modify a noun that follows, just as an English adjective does. Notice that for some of the words, the English translation is adjusted slightly to fit this context.

Examples

shizukana heya / **quiet room**

kireina hana / **pretty flowers**

genkina hito / **healthy person**

benrina dōgu / **convenient tool**

shinsetsuna sensei / **kind teacher**

yūmeina joyū / **famous actress**

jōzuna kashu / **talented singer**

hetana untenshu / **bad driver**

damena hito / **no good person, bad person**

sukina tabemono / **favorite food**

fubenna jikan / **inconvenient time**

iroirona kuni / **various countries**

shōjikina seijika / **honest politician**

teineina aisatsu / **polite greetings**

Tip	This noun modifier construction is similar in form to that of the noun + *no* + noun pattern used to make compound nouns (see **§4.8**): *eigo no sensei* / **English teacher**, etc. With the adjectival nouns, of course, *-na* is used instead of *no*. Otherwise, the pattern is the same. This is one of the noun-like characteristics of the adjectival nouns.

Now look at some examples of this usage in sentences.

Examples

Shizukana heya ga | hoshii desu. | / **I want a quiet room.**

quiet   room   want

Sushi wa, watakushi no sukina tabemono desu. / **Sushi is my favorite food.**

favorite   food

Sore wa fubenna jikan desu. / **That's an inconvenient time.**

inconvenient time

Iroirona   kuni   ni ikimashita. / **I have visited various countries.**

various countries   visited

§8.3–2 Predicate Forms

> The adjectival nouns form a predicate as nouns do, by adding the appropriate form of the copula, *desu* / **is, equals** (see **§7.6** and **§8.3–4**).

Here are the basic forms of *desu*:

desu / is, equals		Affirmative	Negative
Present	Plain	da	dewa nai
	Polite	desu	dewa arimasen
Past	Plain	datta	dewa nakatta
	Polite	deshita	dewa arimasen deshita
Presumptive (Probable)	Plain	darō	dewa nai darō
	Polite	deshō	dewa nai deshō

The following examples illustrate how the adjectival nouns plus a form of *desu* constitute the predicate.

Examples

Kono heya wa, shizuka desu. / **This room is quiet.**

room   quiet

Kōen wa, kirei dewa arimasen deshita. / **The park wasn't pretty.**

park   pretty   wasn't

Chichi wa, genki desu. / **My father is healthy.**

father   healthy

Ano hito wa, supōtsu ga heta desu. / **She isn't good at sports.**

sports   isn't good at

Ano | yakyū no senshu | wa, yūmei desu. / **That baseball player is famous.**

baseball player   famous

Sakana wa, | suki dewa arimasen. | / **I don't like fish. (Fish isn't likable.)**

fish   don't like

Jon san wa, Nihon ga suki desu. / **John likes Japan. (To John, Japan is likable.)**

Niku wa | dame desu. | / **I don't eat meat. (Meat is no good.)**

meat   is no good

§8.3–3 Adverbial Forms

To form adverbs from the *-na* adjectives, use the particle *ni* after the adjective.

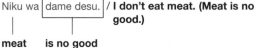

-na Adjective	Adverb
shizuka / **quiet**	shizuka ni / **quiet, quietly**
kirei / **pretty**	kirei ni / **pretty**
genki / **healthy, well**	genki ni / **healthy, well**
shinsetsu / **kind**	shinsetsu ni / **kindly**
teinei / **polite**	teinei ni / **politely**
jōzu / **good at**	jōzu ni / **good at, well**

Look at the adverbial forms in sentences. They are often used with the verbs *naru* / **become** and *suru* / **do**.

Examples

Kanojo wa, | shizuka ni | arukimasu. / **She walks quietly.**

quietly   walks

Ano hito wa, | teinei ni | hanashimashita. / **He spoke politely.**

politely   spoke

Kanja wa, | genki ni | narimashita. / **The patient became healthy.**

healthy   became

Satō san wa, eigo ga | jōzu ni | narimashita. / **Ms. Sato became good at English.**

good at

Satō san wa, eigo o | jōzu ni | hanashimasu. / **Mr. Sato speaks English well.**

well   speaks

Shizuka ni shinasai. / **Please be quiet.**

quiet   do

§8.3-4 Adjectival Noun Charts

In the following charts you will find predicate forms of a sample of adjectival nouns.

kirei / **beautiful**

Stem: kirei		Adjectival Noun	
		Affirmative	Negative
Present:	Plain	kirei da	kirei dewa nai
			kirei ja nai
	Polite	kirei desu	kirei dewa arimasen
			kirei ja arimasen
Past:	Plain	kirei datta	kirei dewa nakatta
			kirei ja nakatta
	Polite	kirei datta desu	kirei dewa nakatta desu
			kirei ja nakatta desu
		kirei deshita	kirei dewa arimasen deshita
			kirei ja arimasen deshita
Gerund (-*te* form)		kireide	kirei dewa nakute
			kirei ja nakute
Presumptive:	Plain	kirei darō	kirei dewa nai darō
			kirei ja nai darō
	Polite	kirei deshō	kirei dewa nai deshō
			kirei ja nai deshō
Conditional:		kirei nara	kirei dewa nai nara
			kirei ja nakereba
		kirei dattara	kirei dewa nakattara
			kirei ja nakattara
		kirei da to	kirei dewa nai to
			kirei ja nai to

suki / **fond of, to like**

Stem: suki			Adjectival Noun
		Affirmative	Negative
Present:	Plain	suki da	suki dewa nai suki ja nai
	Polite	suki desu	suki dewa arimasen suki ja arimasen
Past:	Plain	suki datta	suki dewa nakatta suki ja nakatta
	Polite	suki datta desu	suki dewa nakatta desu suki ja nakatta desu
		suki deshita	suki dewa arimasen deshita suki ja arimasen deshita
Gerund (-*te* form)		sukide	suki dewa nakute suki ja nakute
Presumptive:	Plain	suki darō	suki dewa nai darō suki ja nai darō
	Polite	suki deshō	suki dewa nai deshō suki ja nai deshō
Conditional:		suki nara	suki dewa nai nara suki ja nakereba
		suki dattara	suki dewa nakattara suki ja nakattara
		suki da to	suki dewa nai to suki ja nai to

§8.4 COMPARISONS

To compare things in Japanese, the adjectives themselves do not change. Instead, there is a special pattern to learn. This pattern works for both -*i* adjectives and -*na* adjectives.

To say **A is bigger than B**, the pattern is as follows:

To say **A is cheaper than B**, the pattern is the same:

Examples

Budō wa, meron yori yasui desu. / **Grapes are cheaper than melons.**

grapes   melons than cheap are

Tōkyō wa, Kyōto yori ōkii desu. / **Tokyo is bigger than Kyoto.**

than big is

Kyōto wa, Tōkyō yori chiisai desu. / **Kyoto is smaller than Tokyo.**

than small is

Tip	To understand clearly which is which in the comparison, the key is the word *yori* / **than.** Focus on this word and the English meaning, and you can quickly sort it out. If you want to say **Oranges are cheaper than apples,** start with **than apples** in English. In Japanese it becomes *ringo yori* / **apples than,** and you can see that **apples** takes the **B** slot in the pattern. The full sentence is as follows:

Orenji wa, ringo   yori yasui desu. / **Oranges are**
       | | | | | **cheaper than**
                                apples.
oranges apples than cheap are

Another phrase is often used with this pattern, although the meaning remains the same. The words are *no hō*, plus the particle *ga*. The *no* is like the possessive particle used to link the nouns with whatever follows, and *hō* can be translated as **side** or **direction.** The pattern looks like this:

Amerika yori, Nihon no hō ga chiisai desu. / **Japan is**
       | | | | | **smaller**
      than   **'s side** **small** **is** **than**
                                America.

Niku   yori, sakana no hō ga oishii desu. / **Fish is**
  | | | | | | | **more**
                             delicious
meat than   fish   's side delicious is **than**
                             meat.

Examples

Shikago to Tōkyō to, dochira ga suki

    or   or which

desu ka. / **Which do you like better, Chicago or Tokyo?**

Tōkyō no hō ga suki desu. / **I like Tokyo better.**

    's side   like is

Jon san to Tomu san to, dare no hō ga wakai

    or   or whose side younger

desu ka. / **Who is younger, John or Tom?**

is

Jon san no hō ga, wakai desu. / **John is younger.**

    's side   young is

Notice the particle and word order changes in the following two sentences. In the first one, *no hō ga* is used, in the second, *yori* is used alone. Both sentences have the same meaning, but including *no hō ga* makes for stronger contrast in the comparison.

Examples

Basu yori, chikatetsu no hō ga benri desu. / **The subway is more convenient than the bus.**

Chikatetsu wa, basu yori benri desu. / **The subway is more convenient than the bus.**

| | | |
subway   bus than

Another way to answer questions about comparisons is with a simple statement.

Examples

Ringo to momo to, dochira ga suki desu ka.

| | | | | | |
apples or peaches or   which   like

/ **Which do you like better, apples or peaches?**

Ringo ga suki desu. / **I like apples better.**

Another option is to use the word *motto*, which means **more**, for emphasis. It connotes **much** (**more, better,** etc.). If you use this with *no hō* ga, the emphasis is even stronger.

Examples

Ringo ga motto suki desu. / **I like apples much more.**

Ringo no hō ga, motto suki desu. / **I like apples much more.**

To convey a superlative meaning, use the word *ichiban* / **most, -est,** etc.

Examples

Dono kudamono ga ichiban suki desu ka. / **Which fruit do you like best?**

| | | | |
| which | fruit | best | like |

Banana ga ichiban suki desu. / **I like bananas best.**

Nihon de wa, dono tsuki ga ichiban samui desu ka.

| | |
| month | cold |

/ **Which month is the coldest in Japan?**

§8.5 NOMINALIZATION

Adjectives can be *nominalized*, or made into nouns, by a simple device for each of the two kinds.

For *-i* adjectives, add *-no* to the basic, or dictionary, form.

-i Adjective	Noun Form
ōkii / **big**	ōkiino / **big one**
atarashii / **new**	atarashiino / **new one**
hayai / **fast**	hayaino / **fast one**
shiroi / **white**	shiroino / **white one**
amai / **sweet**	amaino / **sweet one**
akai / **red**	akaino / **red one**
kiiroi / **yellow**	kiiroino / **yellow one**

As with English, this form usually occurs in a context, that is, answering a question, or referring to something mutually understood.

Examples

Ringo o kudasai. / **I want some apples.**

Akaino	to	kiiroino	to,	dochira	ga ii desu ka.
red ones	**or**	**yellow ones**	**or**	**which**	

/ **Which do you want, red ones or yellow ones?**

Look at two ways of saying the same thing. Note the difference in emphasis.

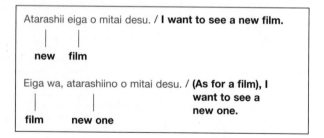

Here are some more examples of nominalized adjectives used in sentences:

Examples

Kēki wa, amaino o kudasai. / **(As for the cake), give me the sweet one.**

| |
cake sweet one

Hoteru no heya wa, chiisaino ga hoshii desu. / **(As for a hotel room), I want a small one.**

| | |
hotel room small one

For -*na* adjectives, add -*no* to the -*na* form.

-*na* Adjective, -*na* Form	Noun Form
shizukana / **quiet**	shizukanano / **quiet one**
kireina / **pretty**	kireinano / **pretty one**
yūmeina / **famous**	yūmeinano / **famous one**
sukina / **like, favorite**	sukinano / **favorite one**
benrina / **convenient**	benrinano / **convenient one**
teineina / **polite**	teineinano / **polite one, politeness**
hetana / **not good at**	hetanano / **unskillful one**

Here are some sentences with these forms. The uses are the same as for the -*i* adjective sentences above.

Examples

Kisha wa, | benrinano | ni | noritai desu. | / **(As for trains), I want to take a convenient one.**

train convenient one want to take

Kireinano ga | ii desu. | / **I want pretty ones.**

pretty ones want

Teineinano wa taisetsu desu. / **Politeness is important.**

politeness important

§9.

Adverbs

§9.1 WHAT ARE ADVERBS?

Adverbs are words which modify or describe verbs, adjectives, or other adverbs. They indicate *time, place, manner*, and *degree*. They answer such questions as **when**, **where**, **how**, and **to what extent**.

As in English, some words in Japanese that are adverbs in one sentence can be a different part of speech in another sentence.

Examples

Kyō Tōkyō ni ikimasu. / **Today I'm going to Tokyo.**

Today

adverb

Kyō wa nichiyōbi desu. / **Today is Sunday.**

Today

noun

§9.2 ADVERBS OF PLACE

Some of the demonstrative pronouns (see §5.5) function as adverbs of place.

> koko / **here**
> soko / **there**
> asoko / **over there**

Examples

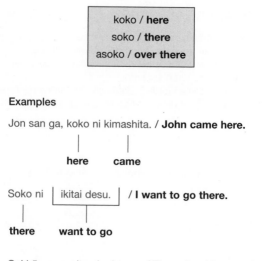

Jon san ga, koko ni kimashita. / **John came here.**

|
here   came

Soko ni | ikitai desu. | / **I want to go there.**
|
there   want to go

Gakkō wa, asoko ni arimasu. / **The school is over there.**
|
school   over there

§9.3 ADVERBS OF TIME

kinō / **yesterday**	maishū / **every week**
kyō / **today**	maitsuki / **every month**
ashita / **tomorrow**	senshū / **last week**
mainichi / **every day**	sengetsu / **last month**
maiasa / **every morning**	raishū / **next week**
maiban / **every night**	raigetsu / **next month**
ima / **now**	kyonen / **last year**
saikin / **recently**	kotoshi / **this year**
yagate / **soon**	rainen / **next year**
sugu / **immediately**	itsuka / **sometime**
mada / **yet, still**	

Examples

Mainichi shinbun o yomimasu. / **I read a newspaper every day.**

every day	**newspaper**	**read**

Sugu | kite kudasai. | / **Please come immediately.**

immediately **please come**

Yūbin wa, mada desu. / **The mail isn't here yet.**

mail **not yet**

Yagate haru ga kimasu. / **Spring will come soon.**

soon **spring** **come**

§9.4 ADVERBS OF MANNER AND DEGREE

As in English, adjectives can be made into adverbs of manner and degree:

Adjective	Adverb
hayai / **quick**	hayaku / **quick, quickly**
warui / **bad**	waruku / **bad, badly**
shizuka / **quiet**	shizuka ni / **quiet, quietly**
shinsetsu / **kind**	shinsetsu ni / **kindly**

See **§8.2–3** and **§8.3–3** for more information on the adverbial forms of adjectives.

Some of the demonstrative pronouns are adverbs of manner (see **§5.5**).

> kō / **this way, like this**
> sō / **that way, like that**
> ā / **that way, like that**
> dō / **how**

Examples

Kō   shimashō. / **Let's do it this way.**
| |
this way   let's do

Sō | shite kudasai. | / **Please do it that way.**
| |
that way   please do

Ā suru to yoku dekimasu. / **If you do it that way, you can do better.**

that way   if   better   can do

Ōsaka ni wa, dō ikimasu ka. / **How do you get to Osaka?**

how   go

Here are some other adverbs of manner and degree

amari / **not much, not often**	sukoshi / **a little, few**
bakari / **only**	tabitabi / **often**
chotto / **a little, for a moment**	tabun / **maybe, perhaps, probably**
dandan / **gradually**	taihen / **very (in the sense of extreme degree, positive or negative), greatly**
futsū / **usually**	
hotondo / **almost, all but, hardly**	
ikaga / **how**	taitei / **generally, mainly, perhaps, probably**
itsumo / **always**	takusan / **a lot**
kitto / **certainly, surely**	tamani / **occasionally**
mata / **again**	tokidoki / **sometimes**
minna / **all**	totemo / **very**
mō / **more, already**	yoku / **well, often, much**
motto / **more**	yukkuri / **slowly**
nakanaka / **quite, rather, completely, at all**	zenzen / **at all (with negative verbs)**
	zuibun / **rather, quite**

Examples

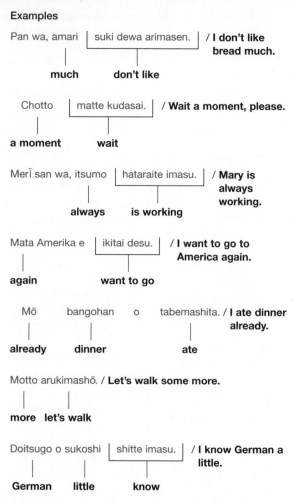

Pan wa, amari | suki dewa arimasen. / **I don't like bread much.**

much   don't like

Chotto | matte kudasai. / **Wait a moment, please.**

a moment   wait

Merī san wa, itsumo | hataraite imasu. / **Mary is always working.**

always   is working

Mata Amerika e | ikitai desu. / **I want to go to America again.**

again   want to go

Mō   bangohan   o   tabemashita. / **I ate dinner already.**

already   dinner   ate

Motto arukimashō. / **Let's walk some more.**

more   let's walk

Doitsugo o sukoshi | shitte imasu. / **I know German a little.**

German   little   know

Taihen | omoshirokatta desu. | / **It was very interesting.**

very   was interesting

Ano hito wa, takusan hanashimasu. / **He talks a lot.**

a lot   talks

Tokidoki Tōkyō ni ikimasu. / **I sometimes go to Tokyo.**

sometimes   go

Totemo | oishikatta desu.   / **It was very delicious.**

very   was delicious

Rokugatsu wa, ame ga yoku furimasu. / **It rains often in June.**

June   rain   often   falls

Yukkuri | hanashite kudasai. | / **Please speak slowly.**

slowly   speak

Eiga wa, zenzen omoshiroku | arimasen deshita. |

movie   at all   Interesting   wasn't

/ **The movie wasn't interesting at all.**

Special Topics

§10.

Numbers

§10.1   CARDINAL NUMBERS

Zero to One Hundred Million

From 1 to 10 only, there are two sets of numbers. The set on the right, of Japanese origin, stops at 10. The set on the left, of Chinese origin, continues indefinitely.

rei	0	
ichi	1	hitotsu
ni	2	futatsu
san	3	mittsu
shi/yon	4	yottsu
go	5	itsutsu
roku	6	muttsu
shichi/nana	7	nanatsu
hachi	8	yattsu
ku/kyū	9	kokonotsu
jū	10	tō

To form numbers from 11 to 19, start with *jū*,10, and then add the number you need from the column on the left in the preceding chart.

11 jūichi	12 jūni	13 jūsan	14 jūshi/yon	15 jūgo
16 jūroku	17 jūshichi / nana		18 jūhachi	19 jūku

The rest is easy. Twenty is two tens, or *ni jū*, and for 21, just add the 1: *ni jū ichi*.

20 nijū	30 sanjū	40 yonjū	50 gojū
21 nijūichi	31 sanjūichi	41 yonjūichi	51 gojūichi
60 rokujū	70 nanajū	80 hachijū	90 kyūjū
61 rokujūichi	71 nanajūichi	81 hachijūichi	91 kyūjūichi

With 100, *hyaku*, and 1,000, *sen*, the pattern is basically the same, but there are some sound changes, as you will see in the chart below:

100	hyaku	1,000	sen
200	nihyaku	2,000	nisen
300	sanbyaku	3,000	sanzen
400	yonhyaku	4,000	yonsen
500	gohyaku	5,000	gosen
600	roppyaku	6,000	rokusen
700	nanahyaku	7,000	nanasen
800	happyaku	8,000	hassen
900	kyūhyaku	9,000	kyūsen

Japanese uses 10,000 as a counting unit. Each unit of 10,000 is called *man*.

So 10,000 is *ichiman*, 20,000 is *niman*, 100,000 is *jūman*, 200,000 is *nijūman*, 1,000,000 is *hyakuman* (100 units of 10,000). This continues until 100,000,000, *ichioku*.

Now for one more set: These days, Japanese often use English cardinal numbers, especially from one to ten. But the pronunciation is somewhat different.

1	wan	6	shikkusu
2	tsū	7	sebun
3	surī	8	eito
4	fō	9	nain
5	faibu	10	ten

§10.2   ORDINAL NUMBERS

The ordinal numbers are formed by adding *banme* to the cardinal numbers.

first	ichibanme	**sixth**	rokubanme
second	nibanme	**seventh**	nanabanme
third	sanbanme	**eighth**	hachibanme
fourth	yonbanme	**ninth**	kyūbanme
fifth	gobanme	**tenth**	jūbanme

To continue, follow the pattern for the cardinal numbers, adding *banme*. **Eleventh** is *jūichibanme*, **twelfth** is *jūnibanme*, and so forth.

Telling Time

To express time in Japanese, we start with a list of the **hours**, then a list of the **minutes**, and then we put them together.

Here are the **hours**:

1 o'clock	ichiji	7 o'clock	shichiji
2 o'clock	niji	8 o'clock	hachiji
3 o'clock	sanji	9 o'clock	kuji
4 o'clock	yoji	10 o'clock	jūji
5 o'clock	goji	11 o'clock	jūichiji
6 o'clock	rokuji	12 o'clock	jūniji

Now the **minutes**:

1 minute	ippun	7 minutes	nanafun
2 minutes	nifun	8 minutes	happun
3 minutes	sanpun	9 minutes	kyūfun
4 minutes	yonpun	10 minutes	juppun
5 minutes	gofun	11 minutes	jūippun
6 minutes	roppun	12 minutes	jūnifun

13 minutes	jūsanpun	21 minutes	nijūippun
14 minutes	jūyonpun	22 minutes	nijūnifun
15 minutes	jūgofun	23 minutes	nijūsanpun
16 minutes	jūroppun	24 minutes	nijūyonpun
17 minutes	jūnanafun	25 minutes	nijūgofun
18 minutes	jūhappun	30 minutes	sanjuppun
19 minutes	jūkyūfun	40 minutes	yonjuppun
20 minutes	nijūppun	50 minutes	gojuppun

Now we can put them together. Say the hour first, then the minutes, then add *desu*:

Examples

Nanji desu ka. / **What time is it?**

Jūji jūgofun desu. / **It's 10:15.**

- Using *sugi*, which means **past** or **after**, is optional.

    Jūji jūgofun   sugi   desu. / **It's 10:15.**

    |

    after

- At 15 minutes before the hour, start using *mae*, which means **to** or **before**.

    Jūji jūgofun mae desu. / **It's a quarter to ten.**

    |

    before

- *Han* means **half**, as in **half past** the hour.

Goji desu.	**It's 5 o'clock.**
Goji gofun desu.	**It's 5:05.**
Goji juppun desu.	**It's 5:10.**
Goji jūgofun desu.	**It's 5:15.**
Goji nijuppun desu.	**It's 5:20.**
Goji nijūgofun desu.	**It's 5:25.**
Goji han desu.	**It's 5:30.**
Goji sanjūgofun desu.	**It's 5:35.**
Goji yonjuppun desu.	**It's 5:40.**
Goji yonjūgofun desu.	**It's 5:45.**
Rokuji jūgofun mae desu.	**It's a quarter to six.**
Rokuji juppun mae desu.	**It's 5:50/ten to six.**
Rokuji gofun mae desu.	**It's 5:55/five to six.**

- *Gozen* is A.M. *Gogo* is P.M. Say them *before* you say the hour.

   Examples

   Gozen kuji desu. / **It's 9 A.M.**

   |

   A.M.

   Gogo jūji desu. / **It's 10 P.M.**

   |

   P.M.

Tip

For time schedules, as in railway and airline timetables, numbers 1 to 59 are used for minutes, *not* **a quarter to** or **ten to** the hour.

Transportation timetables are based on the 24-hour clock. Airline and train schedules are expressed in terms of a point within a 24-hour sequence.

Examples

Watakushi no kisha wa, jūsanji yonjūhappun ni demasu.
/ **My train departs at 13:48.**

Watakushi no hikōki wa, jūji gojūsanpun ni tsukimasu.
/ **My plane arrives at 10:53.**

Tip

Japanese like to keep precise time. So even for an approximation, they prefer to use a narrower range of time.

Examples:

- Jūji jūnana fun goro, Ōsaka de jishin ga arimashita. / **There was an earthquake in Osaka around 10:17.**
- Hoteru made takushī de nijū nana fun gurai kakarimasu. / **It takes about 27 minutes to the hotel by taxi.**

§12.

Classifiers

To count things in Japanese, you use special classifiers, or counters. Here are some of the most common ones:

Counting Different Kinds of Things

People				
1 hitori	2 futari	3 sannin	4 yonin	5 gonin
6 rokunin	7 nananin	8 hachinin	9 kunin	10 jūnin

Long, thin objects (pencils, bottles, trees, etc.)				
1 ippon	2 nihon	3 sanbon	4 yonhon	5 gohon
6 roppon	7 nanahon	8 happon	9 kyūhon	10 jūppon

Bound objects (books, magazines, notebooks, etc.)				
1 issatsu	2 nisatsu	3 sansatsu	4 yonsatsu	5 gosatsu
6 rokusatsu	7 nanasatsu	8 hassatsu	9 kyūsatsu	10 jussatsu

Thin, flat objects (paper, bills, cloth, tickets, dishes, etc.)				
1 ichimai	2 nimai	3 sanmai	4 yomai	5 gomai
6 rokumai	7 nanamai	8 hachimai	9 kyūmai	10 jūmai

Liquid or dry measures (glasses or cups of water, coffee, tea, etc.)

1 ippai	2 nihai	3 sanbai	4 yonhai	5 gohai
6 roppai	7 nanahai	8 happai	9 kyūhai	10 juppai

Houses, buildings, etc.

1 ikken	2 niken	3 sangen	4 yonken	5 goken
6 rokken	7 nanaken	8 hakken	9 kyūken	10 jukken

Floors of buildings

1 ikkai	2 nikai	3 sangai	4 yonkai	5 gokai
6 rokkai	7 nanakai	8 hakkai	9 kyūkai	10 jukkai

Animals, fish, insects

1 ippiki	2 nihiki	3 sanbiki	4 yonhiki	5 gohiki
6 roppiki	7 nanahiki	8 happiki	9 kyūhiki	10 juppiki

Small objects not in categories listed above (apples, candy, etc.)

1 ikko / hitotsu	2 niko / futatsu	3 sanko / mittsu
4 yonko / yottsu	5 goko / itsutsu	6 rokko / muttsu
7 nanako / nanatsu	8 hakko / yattsu	9 kyūko / kokonotsu
10 jukko / tō		

Examples

hito futari / **two people**

inu sanbiki / **three dogs**

hito futari to inu sanbiki / **two people and three dogs**

Tēburu no ue niwa, orenji ga mittsu to hon ga nisatsu
arimasu. / **Three oranges and two books are on
the table.**

Kōen niwa, hito ga nananin to inu ga gohiki imasu. / **Seven
people and five dogs are in the park.**

> **Tip**
>
> To form the question word for the classifiers, do
> the following:
>
> - Start with the word for counting three of
>   anything.
> - Instead of *san*, use *nan*.
>
> For example:
> *sangen* becomes *nangen*/**how many houses,
> buildings, etc.**
> *sanbai* becomes *nanbai*/**how many glasses,
> cups, etc.**

Examples

Tanaka san wa enpitsu o nanbon kaimashita ka. / **How many
pencils did Mr. Tanaka buy?**

Gohon kaimashita. / **He bought five pencils.**

§13.

Days, Months, Seasons, the Weather

§13.1 DAYS OF THE WEEK

getsuyōbi / **Monday**	mokuyōbi / **Thursday**
kayōbi / **Tuesday**	kinyōbi / **Friday**
suiyōbi / **Wednesday**	doyōbi / **Saturday**

nichiyōbi / **Sunday**

asa / **morning** gogo / **afternoon**

yūgata / **evening** yoru / **night**

Related Expressions

Kyō wa, nani yōbi desu ka. / **What day is today?**

Kyō wa, _____ desu. / **It's _____.**

ichinichi / **a day**	konshū / **this week**
kyō / **today**	raishū / **next week**
kinō / **yesterday**	senshū / **last week**
ototoi / **the day before yesterday**	isshūkan / **for one week**
ashita / **tomorrow**	nishūkan / **for two weeks**
asatte / **the day after tomorrow**	yūgata / **in the early evening**
	yoru / **in the evening, at night**
shū / **week**	asa made ni / **by morning**

kayōbi made ni / **by Tuesday**

futsuka kan / **for two days**

ichi nichi de / **in one day**

futsuka de / **in two days**

isshūkan de / **in one week**

nishūkan de / **in two weeks**

mikka mae / **three days ago**

kesa / **this morning**

kyō no gogo / **this afternoon**

konban / **tonight, this evening**

ashita no ban / **tomorrow night**

gozen chū / **in the morning**

gogo / **in the afternoon**

hiru ni / **at noon**

heijitsu / **weekday**

shūmatsu / **weekend**

yasumi / **day off**

kyūjitsu / **holiday**

shigoto bi / **work day**

mainichi / **every day**

kyō kara isshūkan go / **a week from today**

kyō kara / **from today on**

ichinichi ni tsuki / **per day**

kyō jū ni / **during the day**

konshū jū ni / **during the week**

§13.2 MONTHS OF THE YEAR

ichigatsu / **January**	shichigatsu / **July**
nigatsu / **February**	hachigatsu / **August**
sangatsu / **March**	kugatsu / **September**
shigatsu / **April**	jūgatsu / **October**
gogatsu / **May**	jūichigatsu / **November**
rokugatsu / **June**	jūnigatsu / **December**

nan gatsu / **which month**

§13.3 DAYS OF THE MONTH

tsuitachi / **1st**	jūrokunichi / **16th**
futsuka / **2nd**	jūshichinichi / **17th**
mikka / **3rd**	jūhachinichi / **18th**
yokka / **4th**	jūkunichi / **19th**
itsuka / **5th**	hatsuka / **20th**
muika / **6th**	nijūichinichi / **21st**
nanoka / **7th**	nijūninichi / **22nd**
yōka / **8th**	nijūsannichi / **23rd**
kokonoka / **9th**	nijūyokka / **24th**
tōka / **10th**	nijūgonichi / **25th**
jūichinichi / **11th**	nijūrokunichi / **26th**
jūninichi / **12th**	nijūshichinichi / **27th**
jūsannichi / **13th**	nijūhachinichi / **28th**
jūyokka / **14th**	nijūkunichi / **29th**
jūgonichi / **15th**	sanjūnichi / **30th**
	sanjūichinichi / **31st**

nan nichi / **which day**

§13.4 COUNTING DAYS

ichinichi / **one day**	nanoka / **seven days**
futsuka / **two days**	yōka / **eight days**
mikka / **three days**	kokonoka / **nine days**
yokka / **four days**	tōka / **ten days**
itsuka / **five days**	jūichinichi / **eleven days**
muika / **six days**	jūninichi / **twelve days**

Related Expressions

Nikagetsu mae / **2 months ago**

sengetsu / **last month**

kongetsu / **this month**

raigetsu / **next month**

_____ gatsu chū ni / **during the month of** _____

_____ gatsu irai / **since the month of** _____

_____ gatsu ni / **for the month of** _____

mai tsuki / **every month**

ikkagetsu ni tsuki / **per month**

ikkagetsu / **one month**

sūkagetsu / **a few months**

Kyō wa, nan nichi desu ka. / **What's today's date?**

Kyō wa, _____ desu. / **Today is _____.**

gogatsu tsuitachi, getsuyōbi / **Monday, May 1**

rokugatsu futsuka, kayōbi / **Tuesday, June 2**

Note: For these expressions, use the days of the month listed in **§13.3**.

§13.5 SEASONS

haru / **spring**	aki / **fall**
natsu / **summer**	fuyu / **winter**

Related Expressions

Haru desu. / **It's spring.**

Natsu desu. / **It's summer.**

Aki desu. / **It's fall.**

Fuyu desu. / **It's winter.**

§13.6 THE WEATHER

Tenki wa dō desu ka. / **How's the weather?**
Samui desu. / **It's cold.**
Totemo samui desu. / **It's very cold.**
Yuki ga futte imasu. / **It's snowing.**
Atatakai desu. / **It's warm.**
Hi ga tette imasu. / **It's sunny.**
Atsui desu. / **It's hot.**
Shikke ga takai desu. / **It's humid.**
Mushiatsui desu. / **It's hot and humid.**
Ii tenki desu. / **It's a beautiful day.**
Ame ga futte imasu. / **It's raining.**
Arashi desu. / **It's stormy.**
Kaminari ga natte, inazuma ga hikatte imasu. / **It's thundering and lightning.**
Suzushii desu. / **It's cool.**
Kiri desu. / **It's foggy.**
Ame ga, hageshiku futte imasu. / **It's raining heavily.**

§14.

Family Relationships

Choose a term from the appropriate column in the chart below when talking about family members. In Japanese, the terms for family relationships differ according to whether you are talking about your own family to someone else, or about the other person's family. You refer to your own family with a set of neutral forms, to another person's family with a set of honorific terms.

Family Member	Talking about Your Family	Talking about Another's Family
grandfather	sofu	ojiisan
grandmother	sobo	obāsan
father	chichi	otōsan
mother	haha	okāsan
husband	otto/shujin	goshujin
wife	tsuma	okusan
uncle	oji	ojisan
aunt	oba	obasan
son	musuko	musukosan
daughter	musume	ojōsan
cousin	itoko	itoko

elder brother	ani	oniisan
younger brother	otōto	otōtosan
elder sister	ane	onēsan
younger sister	imōto	imōtosan
grandchild	mago	omagosan
nephew	oi	oigosan
niece	mei	meigosan

Within Japanese families with children, you may often hear the words "papa" and "mama" used as well as the traditional terms.

§15.

Useful Words and Phrases

You will find this section useful in communicating with the Japanese. Just find the category you want, and choose the expression you need!

§15.1 GREETINGS

To begin, you should know that Japanese does not have a word that is the equivalent of the English word **Hello**. Instead, use the words for **Good morning, Good afternoon**, etc.

Ohayō gozaimasu. / **Good morning.**

Konnichiwa. / **Good afternoon.**

Konbanwa. / **Good evening.**

Oyasuminasai. / **Good night.** (This is used at the end of the evening, or at bedtime.)

Sayōnara. / **Goodbye.**

Japanese has no equivalent for the English expression **How are you?** that is used as a daily greeting. The following expression is used only when you have not seen someone for a while.

> Ogenki desu ka. / **How are you?**
> Hai, okagesama de. / **Fine, thank you.**

§15.2 COMMON EXPRESSIONS

You will find these expressions handy in daily life.

Hai. / **Yes.**

Iie. / **No.**

san / **Mr., Mrs., Miss, Ms.**

Dōmo arigatō. / **Thank you.**

Iie, dō itashimashite. / **You're welcome.**

Sumimasen. / **Excuse me** (to get someone's attention).

Gomennasai. / **I'm sorry** (apology).

Onegai shimasu. / **Please** (request).

Dōzo. / **Please** (go ahead, begin).

Moshi moshi. / **Hello.** (This is used for telephone calls, or for getting someone's attention.)

Sumimasen ga. / **Pardon me, but ____.**

Daijōbu desu. / **It's all right.**

Yorokonde. / **With pleasure.**

Mā mā desu. / **So so.**

Itsumo. / **Always.**

Tokidoki. / **Sometimes.**

Hotondo. / **Rarely.**

Ii desu yo. / **I don't mind.**

Ā, sō desu ka. / **Oh, I see.**

Ikimashō ka. / **Shall we go?**

Sā. / **Let's (go/eat/etc.)**

Iie, kekkō desu. / **No, thank you.**

Sō da to omoimasu. / **I think so.**

Sō omoimasen. / **I don't think so.**

Omoshiroi desu. / **It's interesting.**

Owarimashita. / **It's over / I'm finished.**

Hai, sō desu. / **Yes, it is.**

Iie, chigaimasu. / **No, it isn't.**

Chotto, matte kudasai. / **Just a moment, please.**

Sugu, onegai shimasu. / **Right away** (request).

Soredewa nochi hodo. / **See you later.** (polite)

Soredewa mata. / **See you later.**

Jā mata. / **See you later.** (casual)

Jā ne. / **See you.** (very casual)

Soredewa mata ashita. / **See you tomorrow.**

Wakarimasu ka. / **Do you understand?**

Hai, wakarimasu. / **Yes, I understand.**

Iie, wakarimasen. / **No, I don't understand.**

Eigo ga wakarimasu ka. / **Do you understand English?**

Nihongo ga, sukoshi hanasemasu. / **I speak a little Japanese.**

Nihongo wa, wakarimasen. / **I don't understand Japanese.**

Mō ichido onegai shimasu. / **Could you repeat it, please?**

Mō sukoshi, yukkuri hanshite kudasai. / **Please speak slowly.**

Eigo o hanashimasu ka. / **Do you speak English?**

Kore wa, Nihongo de nan to iimasu ka. / **What's this called in Japanese?**

Kore wa, nan to iimasu ka. / **What do you call this?**

Sumimasen ga, tasukete itadakemasen ka. / **Excuse me, could you help me, please?**

§15.3   SOME QUESTIONS AND QUESTION WORDS

Dō ka, shimashita ka. / **What's the matter?**

Kore wa, nan desu ka. / **What's this?**

Itsu. / **When?**

Doko. / **Where?**

Doko e. / **Where (are you going)?** (casual)

Naze. / Dōshite. / **Why?**

Dare. / Donata. / **Who?**

Dore. / Dochira. / **Which?**

Nani. / **What?**

Dono kurai. / **How much?**

Ikura. / **How much (money)?**

§15.4   YOUR PERSONAL CONDITION

> Nodo ga, kawaite imasu. / **I'm thirsty.**
>
> Onaka ga, suite imasu. / **I'm hungry.**
>
> Onaka ga, ippai desu. / **I'm full.**
>
> Tsukarete imasu. / **I'm tired.**
>
> Nemui desu. / **I'm sleepy.**
>
> Byōki desu. / **I'm sick.**
>
> Genki desu. / **I'm fine.**
>
> Daijōbu desu. / **I'm all right.**

§15.5   INTRODUCTIONS

Tip	Proper introductions are important in Japan. When possible, it's preferable to have a Japanese friend introduce you to another Japanese. If not, you will find the expressions you need below.

Ano kata wa, donata desu ka. / **Who is that?**

Ano kata wa, donata ka gozonji desu ka. / **Do you know who that is?**

Ano kata ni, ome ni kakaritai no desu ga. / **I would like to meet him / her.**

Ano kata ni, shōkai shite itadakemasen ka. / **Would you introduce me to him / her?**

Totsuzen shitsurei desu ga, jiko shōkai shitemo yoroshii desu ka. / **Pardon me, may I introduce myself?**

Watakushi no namae wa ___ desu. / **My name is ___**

Onamae o ukagaemasu ka. / **May I ask your name?**

Onamae wa. / **What's your name?**

Hajimemashite. Dōzo yoroshiku. / **How do you do?**

Hajimemashite. Kochira koso yoroshiku. / **How do you do?** (reply)

Ome ni kakarete, kōei desu. / **I'm honored to meet you.**

Yoroshiku onegai shimasu. / **I'm glad to meet you.**

meishi / **business card**

Meishi o dōzo. / **Here's my card.**

Arigatō gozaimasu. / **Thank you very much.**

Watakushi no mo dōzo. / **Here's mine.**

Meishi o chōdai dekimasu ka. / **May I have your card?**

Kore ga watakushi no denwa bangō desu. / **This is my telephone number.**

Kore ga watakushi no keitai no bangō desu. / **This is my cell phone number.**

Kore ga watakushi no mēru adoresu desu. / **This is my e-mail address.**

Denwa bangō / keitai no bangō / mēru adoresu o chōdai dekimasu ka. / **May I have your telephone number / cell phone number / e-mail address?**

§16.

Borrowed Words

Countless words borrowed from English are in everyday use in Japan. But even for an English speaker, there are pitfalls. Why? With borrowed words in Japan, you can never assume that they have made the trip across the Pacific intact.

Trust These!

Tip	These words *are* what they seem. If you can understand the pronunciation, you have the meaning.

orenji / **orange**	bīru / **beer**
kōhī / **coffee**	pinku / **pink**
poketto / **pocket**	gasorin / **gasoline**
takushī / **taxi**	basu / **bus**
rajio / **radio**	tomato / **tomato**
banana / **banana**	batā / **butter**
kukkī / **cookie**	sūpu / **soup**
reinkōto / **raincoat**	beddo / **bed**

Careful!

Tip	Some element in each of these words connects it to the original meaning.

pasokon / **personal computer**

waishatsu / **dress shirt**

sūpā / **supermarket**

basuke / **basketball**

puro / **professional**

depāto / **department store**

hankachi / **handkerchief**

irasuto / **illustration**

amefuto / **American football**

ama / **amateur**

netto / **Internet**

nabi / **navigation, navigation system**

Made in Japan!

Tip	With words like these, all bets are off. Don't even think of them as coming from English. How different *are* they? If you are invited for *mōningu baikingu*, don't put on your biking clothes. You are going for a smorgasbord breakfast, *not* morning biking!

baikingu / **smorgasbord** (Viking)

mōningu baikingu / **smorgasbord breakfast**

mōningu sābisu / **breakfast special**

kēki baikingu / **dessert smorgasbord**

manshon / **condominium, modern apartment**

manshon rifōmu / **condominium renovations**

wanpīsu / **dress** (one piece)

ōdāmēdo / **custom-made** / (order made)

merumaga / **e-mail newsletter, blog** / (e-mail magazine)

> Here are some more borrowed words. The meaning in parentheses lets you see the origin. Enjoy them, but remember the tips you have just seen!

anime / **animation**

baburu (keizai) / **bubble economy**

bakansu / **vacation** / (*vacances*—French)

bea / **wage hike** / (base-up)

bebī kā / **baby carrier** / (baby car)

chiketto / **ticket** / (ticket)

defure supairaru / **deflationary spiral**

dejikame / **digital camera**

enerugisshu / **energetic**

esute / **total beauty care** / (*esthetique*—French)

furī daiyaru / **toll-free service** / (free dial)

furītā / **free-lancer** / (free + *Arbeiter*—German)

furonto / **front desk, reception desk** / (front)

kānabi / **car navigation system**

koin randorī / **laundromat** / (coin laundry)

konbini / **convenience store**

konsento / **electrical outlet** / (consent)

masukomi / **mass media** / (mass communication)

meiku / **makeup**

mōningu kōru / **wake-up call** / (morning call)

nanbā disupurei / **caller ID** / (number display)

nego / **negotiation**

nēru / **manicure** / (nail)

nōsurību / **sleeveless** / (no sleeve)

nōto pasokon / **notebook computer**

ōtobai / **motorcycle** / (auto bicycle)

panku / **flat tire** / (puncture)

pansuto / **pantyhose** / (panty stockings)

pāto / **part-time job** / (part)

penki / **paint** / (paint)

pokeberu / **beeper** / (pocket bell)

poruno / **pornography**

rafu / **casual (fashion)** / (rough)

reji / **cashier, checkout counter** / (cash register)

reshipi / **recipe**

rifōmu / **alteration, renovation** / (reform)

rinyūaru / **store renovation** / (renewal)

risutora / **restructuring of business** / (restructuring)

sekuhara / **sexual harassment**

serebu / **celebrity** / (celebrity)

shīru / **sticker** / (seal)

sumaho / **smart phone** / (smart phone)

sumāto / **stylish, slim** / (smart)

supakon / **supercomputer**

toranpu / **playing cards** / (trump)

uirusu / **virus**

wakuchin / **vaccine**

wan puraisu shoppu / **dollar shop** / (one-price shop)

wanrūmu manshon / **studio apartment** / (one-room mansion)

zenekon / **general contractor**

§17.

Synonyms

Synonyms are words with the same or nearly the same meaning.

aruku / ayumu / **to walk**

benkyō suru / manabu / **to study**

betsu no / chigatta / **different**

chōshoku / asagohan / **breakfast**

chūshoku / hirugohan / **lunch**

daidokoro / okatte / **kitchen**

denwa suru / denwa o kakeru / **to telephone**

depāto / hyakkaten / **department store**

furoba / yokushitsu / **bathroom**

gaikoku / ikoku / **foreign country**

genzai / ima / **now**

hajime / saisho / **beginning**

hashiru / kakeru / **to run**

hataraku / shigoto suru / **to work**

henna / okashina / **strange**

hōkō / hōgaku / **direction**

honya / shoten / **bookstore**

iku / mukau / **to go**

isu / koshikake / **chair**

itsumo / tsune ni / **always**

jisho / jiten / **dictionary**

junbi suru / yōi suru / **to prepare**

kaeru / modoru / **to return**

kaiko sareru / kubi ni naru / **to be fired**

katazukeru / seiton suru / **to clean up**

kau / kōnyū suru / **to buy**

keikan / omawarisan / **police officer**

keredomo / dakedo / **but**

keshiki / fūkei / **scenery**

kesshin suru / ketsui suru / **to decide**

ki o tsukeru / chūi suru / **to be careful**

kireina / utsukushii / **beautiful**

komu / konzatsu suru / **to be crowded**

kūkō / hikōjō / **airport**

kuruma / jidōsha / **car**

kyonen / sakunen / **last year**

mata / futatabi / **again**

michi / dōro / **road**

muzukashii / konnan na / **difficult**

nakusu / ushinau / **to lose**

nedan / kakaku / **price**

Nihon ryōri / washoku / **Japanese food**

otearai / toire / **toilet**

otozureru / hōmon suru / **to visit**

owari / saigo / **ending**

seiyō ryōri / yōshoku / **western food**

sensei / kyōshi / **teacher**

shikujiru / shippai suru / **to fail**

shinsetsuna / yasashii / **kind**

shōrai / mirai / **future**

shuppatsu suru / deru / **to depart**

sotto / shizuka ni / **quietly**

sugu ni / tadachi ni / **immediately**

tabi / ryokō / **travel**

tada no / muryō no / **free (cost)**

tasu / kuwaeru / **to add**

tōchaku suru / tsuku / **to arrive**

tomaru / shukuhaku suru / **to stay (overnight)**

totemo / hijō ni / **very**

tozan / yamanobori / **mountain climbing**

uchi / ie / **house**

wakaru / rikai suru / **to understand**

waribiku / makeru / **to discount**

yakkyoku / kusuriya / **pharmacy**

yamai / byōki / **illness**

yasumu / kyūkei suru / **to rest**

yoake / akegata / **dawn**

yūshoku / bangohan / **dinner**

§18.

Antonyms

Antonyms are words with opposite meanings.

agaru / **to rise**	sagaru / **to fall**
akarui / **bright**	kurai / **dark**
anshin suru / **to feel relieved**	shinpai suru / **to worry**
asobu / **to play**	hataraku / **to work**
atsui / **hot (weather)**	samui / **cold (weather)**
atsui / **hot**	tsumetai / **cold**
atsui / **thick**	usui / **thin**
futoi / **thick**	hosoi / **thin**
gen-in / **cause**	kekka / **result**
genki / **well**	byōki / **ill**
hajimaru / **to begin**	owaru / **to end**
hashiru / **to run**	aruku / **to walk**
hayai / **early**	osoi / **late**
hayai / **fast**	osoi / **slow**
hirou / **to pick up**	suteru / **to discard**
ii / **good**	warui / **bad**
jōzu / **good at**	heta / **poor at**
juyō / **demand**	kyōkyū / **supply**
katai / **hard**	yawarakai / **soft**
kiru / **to put on**	nugu / **to take off**
kubaru / **to distribute**	atsumeru / **to collect**

mada / **(not) yet**	mō / **already**
manabu / **to study**	asobu / **to play**
mitsukeru / **to find**	nakusu / **to lose**
nagai / **long**	mijikai / **short**
noboru / **to climb**	kudaru / **to descend**
noru / **to get on**	oriru / **to get off**
okiru / **to get up**	neru / **to go to sleep**
omoi / **heavy**	karui / **light**
omoshiroi / **interesting**	tsumaranai / **boring**
onaji / **same**	chigau / **different**
sansei suru / **to agree**	hantai suru / **to oppose**
seikō suru / **to succeed**	shippai suru / **to fail**
shizuka / **quiet**	urusai / **noisy**
shuppatsu suru / **to depart**	tōchaku suru / **to arrive**
surudoi / **sharp**	nibui / **dull**
takai / **high**	hikui / **low**
takai / **expensive**	yasui / **cheap**
tanjun / **simple**	fukuzatsu / **complicated**
tatsu / **to stand up**	suwaru / **to sit down**
tsukeru / **to turn on**	kesu / **to turn off**
warau / **to laugh**	naku / **to cry**
yasashii / **easy**	muzukashii / **difficult**
yorokobu / **to be pleased**	kanashimu / **to be sad**

§19.
Short Vowel, Long Vowel

Although the words in the two columns look alike, a closer look shows those on the right contain one or more long vowel. Hold these vowel sounds twice as long as the short vowels.

goi / **vocabulary**	gōi / **agreement**
jōho / **concession**	jōhō / **information**
josei / **woman**	jōsei / **situation**
kaigo / **care**	kaigō / **meeting**
kokyō / **hometown**	kōkyō / **public**
koritsu / **isolation**	kōritsu / **publicly funded**
koru / **to get into**	kōru / **to freeze**
koshō / **breakdown**	kōshō / **negotiation**
koten / **classic**	kōten / **improvement**
kuki / **stem**	kūki / **air**
kutsu / **shoe**	kutsū / **pain**
kyoka suru / **to permit**	kyōka suru / **to strengthen**
roka suru / **to filter**	rōka suru / **to age**
sato / **village**	satō / **sugar**
seito / **student**	seitō / **political party**
sekai / **world**	seikai / **correct answer**
shochi suru / **to deal with**	shōchi suru / **to consent**
shōjo / **young girl**	shōjō / **symptoms**
shoka / **early summer**	shōka / **digestion**

shoki no / **early**	shōki no / **sane**
shomei suru / **to sign**	shōmei suru / **to prove**
soshiki / **organization**	sōshiki / **funeral**
suji / **plot**	sūji / **figure**
teki / **enemy**	teiki / **regular**
tokei / **clock**	tōkei / **statistics**
toki / **time**	tōki / **registration**
toru / **to take**	tōru / **to go through**
toshi / **year**	tōshi / **investment**
tsuchi / **soil**	tsūchi / **notice**
yoji / **four o'clock**	yōji / **business**
yuki / **snow**	yūki / **courage**
yume / **dream**	yūmei / **famous**

§20.

Double Consonants

Although the words in the two columns look similar, those on the right contain a double consonant. Don't say the consonant twice: just hold the sound twice as long.

boshū suru / **to recruit**	bosshū suru / **to confiscate**
buka / **subordinate**	bukka / **prices**
bushi / **samurai**	busshi / **goods**
dakai suru / **to break through**	dakkai suru / **to regain**
fukyū suru / **to become widespread**	fukkyū suru / **to be restored**
futō / **unfair**	futtō / **boiling**
gashō / **art dealer**	gasshō / **chorus**
gekō suru / **to leave school**	gekkō suru / **to be enraged**
haken suru / **to dispatch**	hakken suru / **to discover**
haki suru / **to cancel**	hakki suru / **to display**
hosa / **assistance**	hossa / **spasm**
ishō / **clothes**	isshō / **lifetime**
jikan / **time**	jikkan / **sense of reality**
jiken / **incident**	jikken / **experiment**
jikō / **matters**	jikkō / **execution**
jitai / **situation**	jittai / **actual condition**
kaki / **summertime**	kakki / **vigor**
keshō / **makeup**	kesshō / **finals**

kokyō / **hometown**	kokkyō / **border**
koshi / **hips**	kosshi / **gist**
maki / **firewood**	makki / **the last stage**
niki / **two terms**	nikki / **diary**
oto / **sound**	otto / **one's own husband**
saka / **slope**	sakka / **writer**
sasuru / **to stroke**	sassuru / **to guess**
satō / **sugar**	sattō / **rush**
seken / **society**	sekken / **soap**
setai / **household**	settai / **entertainment**
shike / **rough seas**	shikke / **humidity**
shiki / **four seasons**	shikki / **lacquerware**
shisaku suru / **to contemplate**	shissaku suru / **to make a mistake**
shishin / **guideline**	shisshin / **fainting**
shoki / **the early stage**	shokki / **tableware**
shushi / **purpose**	shusshi / **investment**
toshin / **downtown**	tosshin / **rush**

§21.

Same Pronunciation, Different Meaning

These words have the same pronunciation but different meanings. Note that they are not homonyms. Although the romaji and hiragana spellings are the same, the kanji, or Japanese characters, are different.

ai / **love** / **indigo blue**

bin / **bottle** / **flight**

en / **yen** / **relation**

ha / **tooth** / **leaf**

hachi / **eight** / **bee** / **bowl**

han / **half** / **seal**

hana / **flower** / **nose**

han-ei / **reflection** / **prosperity**

hi / **fire** / **day**

jūtai / **delay** / **seriously ill**

kai / **shellfish** / **meeting**

kaji / **housekeeping** / **fire**

kakeru / **to hang** / **to run**

kami / **paper** / **hair**

kanki / **joy** / **cold air**

kawa / **leather** / **river**

kaze / **wind** / **cold**

ken / **ticket / prefecture**

ki / **spirit / tree**

kiji / **article / cloth**

kikai / **opportunity / machine**

kiku / **to listen to / to be effective**

kōgyō / **industry / mining**

kōtei / **school yard / affirmation**

kumo / **cloud / spider**

kyōchō suru / **to emphasize / to coordinate**

me / **eye / bud**

nami / **wave / ordinary**

sasu / **to point out / to sting**

shima / **island / stripe**

shita / **under / tongue**

teichō / **polite / sluggish**

tomaru / **to stay (overnight) / to stop**

utsu / **to hit / to shoot**

utsusu / **to transfer / to photograph**

§22.

Pitch Accent: Different Pitch, Different Meaning

English uses stress, or emphasis, to accent syllables; Japanese uses pitch, or tone. The standard dialect has two pitch levels, high and low. For the English speaker learning Japanese, this takes practice. The lists below show you one aspect of how pitch accent works. On the left, pronounce the syllables at about the same level. On the right, use a higher pitch, or tone, for the capitalized syllables. This difference in pitch results in a different meaning.

aki	(ah-kee) / **autumn**	(ah-KEE) / **vacancy**
ame	(ah-meh) / **candy**	(AH-meh) / **rain**
asa	(ah-sah) / **morning**	(ah-SAH) / **linen**
fuku	(foo-koo) / **to wipe**	(FOO-koo) / **to blow**
haku	(hah-koo) / **to put on**	(HAH-koo) / **to vomit**
hashi	(hah-shee) / **end**	(HAH-shee) / **chopsticks**
		(hah-SHEE) / **bridge**
ima	(ee-mah) / **now**	(ee-MAH) / **living room**
jiku	(jee-koo) / **axis**	(JEE-koo) / **words and phrases**
kakeru	(kah-keh-roo) / **to lack**	(kah-KEH-roo) / **to gamble**
kaki	(kah-kee) / **persimmon**	(KAH-kee) / **oyster**
kami	(kah-mee) / **paper**	(KAH-mee) / **god**
	(kah-mee) / **hair**	

kari	(kah-ree) / **debt**	(KAH-ree) **hunting**
kau	(kah-oo) / **to buy**	(KAH-oo) / **to keep**
kiru	(kee-roo) / **to cut**	(kee-ROO) / **to put on**
kisha	(kee-shah) / **train**	(KEE-shah) / **reporter**
michi	(mee-chee) / **street**	(MEE-chee) / **unknown**
momo	(moh-moh) / **peach**	(MOH-moh) / **thigh**
muku	(moo-koo) / **to peel**	(MOO-koo) / **pure**
mushi	(moo-shee) / **insect**	(MOO-shee) / **disregard**
nasu	(nah-soo) / **eggplant**	(NAH-soo) / **to achieve**
neru	(neh-roo) / **to go to bed**	(NEH-roo) / **to refine (a plan)**
sake	(sah-keh) / *sake*	(SAH-keh) / **salmon**
saku	(sah-koo) / **to bloom**	(SAH-koo) / **to tear up**
seki	(seh-kee) / **seat**	(seh-KEE) / **cough**
shiro	(shee-roh) / **white**	(shee-ROH) / **castle**
soba	(soh-bah) / **side**	(SOH-bah) / **buckwheat noodles**
toshi	(toh-shee) / **age**	(TOH-shee) / **city**

Japanese-English Vocabulary

Abbreviations: (adj.) adjective; (adv.) adverb; (conj.) conjunction; (excl.) exclamation; (n.) noun; (p.) particle; (ph.) phrase; (pron.) pronoun; (v.) verb.

ā (adv.), (pron.), **in that manner, like that, that way**
achira (adv.), (pron.) **there, that**
ageru (v.) **to give**
ageru (v.) **to raise**
aisatsu (n.) **greeting**
akai (adj.) **red**
akarui (adj.) **bright**
aki (n.) **autumn**
aku (v.) **to open**
amai (adj.) **sweet**
amari (adv.) **not much, not often**
ame (n.) **rain**
amu (v.) **to knit**
anata (pron.) **you**
anatagata (pron.) **you (polite)**
anatatachi (pron.) **you (plural)**
ane (n.) **elder sister (one's own)**
anime (n.) **animation**
anna (adj.) **that kind of**
ano (adj.) **that**
ano hito (ph.) **that person**
ano hitotachi (ph.) **those persons**
ano kata (ph.) **that person (polite)**
ano katatachi (ph.) **those persons (polite)**
apāto (n.) **apartment**
arau (v.) **to wash**

are (pron.) **that**
aru (v.) **(there) is/are, to be located, to exist, to have**
aruku (v.) **to walk**
asa (n.) **morning**
asatte (n.) **the day after tomorrow**
ashi (n.) **foot**
ashita (adv.), (n.) **tomorrow**
asoko (adv.), (pron.) **over there**
atama (n.) **head**
atarashii (adj.) **new**
ato (n.) **after, the following**
atsui (adj.) **hot**
au (v.) **to meet, to see**

baikingu (n.) **smorgasbord** (Viking)
bakari, bakkari (adv.) **only**
banana (n.) **banana**
bangō (n.) **number**
bangohan (n.) **dinner**
basu (n.) **bus**
batā (n.) **butter**
benkyō suru (v.) **to study**
benri (adj.) **convenient**
biru (n.) **building**
bōeki gaisha (n.) **trading company**
bōnasu (n.) **bonus**
budō (n.) **grapes**
byōki (n.) **illness, sickness**

239

chichi (n.) **father (one's own)**
chiisai (adj.) **small**
chikatetsu (n.) **subway**
chizu (n.) **map**
chotto (adv.) **a little, for a moment**
Chūgokugo (n.) **Chinese (language)**

da (v.) **to be, plain form of desu**
dakara (conj.) **so, also**
dakedo (conj.) **but**
dame (adj.) **no good**
dandan (adv.) **gradually**
dare (pron.) **who**
dareka (pron.) **someone**
daremo (pron.) **no one**
dasu (v.) **to take out**
de (p.) **among, at, from, made from, made of, of, within**
dejikame (n.) **digital camera**
dekakeru (v.) **to go out**
dekiru (v.) **to be able**
demo (conj.) **but**
denki (n.) **light**
denwa (n.) **telephone**
depāto (n.) **department store**
desu (v.) **is, are**
dō (adv.), (pron.) **how**
doa (n.) **door**
dochira (pron.) **where, which (direction, preference)**
dōgu (n.) **tool**
Doitsugo (n.) **German (language)**
doko (pron.) **where (place)**
dokoka (pron.) **somewhere**
dokomo (pron.) **nowhere**
donata (pron.) **which person (polite)**
donataka (pron.) **someone (polite)**
donatamo (pron.) **no one (polite)**
donna (pron.), (adj.) **what kind of**
dore (pron.) **which (persons, things)**

doreka (pron.) **something**
doremo (pron.) **nothing**
dōshite (pron.) **why**
doyōbi (n.) **Saturday**

e (p.) **to, toward**
ebi (n.) **shrimp**
eiga (n.) **movie**
eigo (n.) **English**
eki (n.) **station**
en (n.) **yen**
enpitsu (n.) **pencil**

fuben (adj.) **inconvenient**
Fujisan (n.) **Mt. Fuji**
Furansugo (n.) **French (language)**
furīdaiyaru (n.) **toll-free service**
furo (n.) **bath**
furonto (n.) **front desk**
furu (v.) **to fall (rain, snow, etc.)**
futoru (v.) **to get fat**
futsū (adv.) **usually**
fuyu (n.) **winter**

ga (p.) **and**
ga (p.) **although, but**
ga (p.) **subject marker**
gaikoku (n.) **foreign country**
gakkō (n.) **school**
ganbaru (v.) **to try hard**
geijutsu (n.) **art**
geijutsuka (n.) **artist**
gēmu (n.) **game**
genki (adj.) **healthy, well**
getsuyōbi (n.) **Monday**
gin (n.) **silver**
gogo (n.) **afternoon**
gohan (n.) **cooked rice, meal**
gohon (n.) **book (polite)**
gokekkon (n.) **marriage (polite)**
gozen (n.) **(in the) morning**

ha (n.) **tooth**
hahaoya (n.) **mother, mothers**
hahaoyatachi (n.) **mothers**

hairu (v.) **to enter**
hajimeru (v.) **to begin**
han (n.) **half past**
hana (n.) **flower**
hanasu (v.) **to speak, to talk**
harau (v.) **to pay**
haru (n.) **spring**
hashi (n.) **chopsticks**
hashiru (v.) **to run**
hataraku (v.) **to work**
hayai (adj.) **early, fast, quick**
hayaku (adv.) **early, quick, quickly**
heta (adj.) **bad at**
heya (n.) **room**
hikui (adj.) **low**
hiragana (n.) *hiragana*, **one kind of Japanese syllabary**
hiroi (adj.) **spacious**
hiru (n.) **noon, daytime**
hito (n.) **person**
hitsuyō (n.) **need**
hodo (p.) **as . . . as, as much as**
hon (n.) **book**
honya (n.) **bookstore, bookstore clerk, bookstore owner**
hoshii (adj.) **need, want**
hoteru (n.) **hotel**
hotondo (adv.) **all but, almost, hardly**
hyōron (n.) **commentary**
hyōronka (n.) **critic**

ichiban (adv.), (n.) **the best, most**
ii (adj.) **good, nice, okay**
iiharu (v.) **to insist**
ikaga (adv.) **how, how about?, would you like?**
ikeru (v.) **can go**
iku (v.) **to go**
ikura (pron.) **how much**
ikuraka (pron.) **some, a little**
ikuramo (pron.) **not much**
ikutsu (pron.) **how many**
ima (adv.), (n.) **now**

imi (n.) **meaning**
imōto (n.) **younger sister**
inu (n.) **dog**
iroiro (adj.) **various**
iru (v.) **to need**
iru (v.) **to be, to exist**
isogashii (adj.) **busy**
isogu (v.) **to hurry**
issho ni (adv.) **together**
isshōkenmei (adv.) **hard**
isshūkan (n.) **a week**
isu (n.) **chair**
itadaku (v.) **to receive (from superiors)**
itai (adj.) **painful**
itsu (pron.) **when**
itsuka (pron.) **sometime**
itsumo (adv.), (pron.) **always**
iu (v.) **to say**

ji (n.) **o'clock**
jikan (n.) **time**
jisho (n.) **dictionary**
jiten (n.) **dictionary**
jōgi (n.) **ruler**
joyū (n.) **actress**

ka (p.) **question marker**
ka (p.) **or**
kado (n.) **corner**
kaeru (v.) **to change**
kaeru (v.) **to return**
kaimono (n.) **shopping**
kaisha (n.) **company**
kaku (v.) **to write**
kamera (n.) **camera**
kameraya (n.) **camera shop, camera shop owner, camera shop clerk**
kami (n.) **paper**
kamu (v.) **to bite**
kan (n.) **period**
Kanada (n.) **Canada**
kane (n.) **money**
kanemochi (n.) **rich person**

kangaeru (v.) **to think**

kanji (n.) *kanji*, **Chinese characters**

kankō (n.) **tour, sightseeing**

kanojo (pron.) **she, her**

kanojora (pron.) **they, them (female)**

kanojotachi (pron.) **they, them (female)**

kantan (adj.) **easy**

kara (p.) **from**

kara (p.) **because, since**

kara (p.) **after, ever since, since**

kare (pron.) **he, him**

karera (pron.) **they, them (all male or male and female)**

kariru (v.) **to borrow**

karui (adj.) **light(weight)**

kasa (n.) **umbrella**

kashu (n.) **singer**

kasu (v.) **to lend**

katakana (n.) *katakana*, **one kind of Japanese syllabary**

kau (v.) **to buy**

kawa (n.) **river**

kayōbi (n.) **Tuesday**

keitai (n.) **cell phone**

kēki (n.) **cake**

kekkon (n.) **marriage**

kekkon suru (v.) **to get married**

keredo (p.) **and**

keredo (p.) **although, but, however**

keredomo (conj.) **but**

ki (n.) **tree, wood**

kiiroi (adj.) **yellow**

kiku (v.) **to hear, to listen, to ask**

kimochi (n.) **feeling**

kinō (adv.), (n.) **yesterday**

kinyōbi (n.) **Friday**

kirei (adj.) **beautiful**

kiru (v.) **to put on (clothing)**

kiru (v.) **to cut**

kisha (n.) **train**

kitto (adv.) **certainly, surely**

kō (adv.), (pron.) **in this manner, like this, this way**

kōcha (n.) **tea**

kochira (adv.), (pron.) **here, this**

kodomo (n.) **child, children**

kodomotachi (n.) **children**

kōen (n.) **park**

kōhī (n.) **coffee**

koko (adv.), (pron.) **here**

kokoa (n.) **cocoa**

komu (v.) **to be crowded**

konbini (n.) **convenience store**

kondo (n.) **this time**

konna (adj.) **this kind of**

kono (adj.) **this, these**

konshū (n.) **this week**

kore (pron.) **this**

kōto (n.) **coat**

kotoshi (n.) **this year**

kudamono (n.) **fruit**

kudasai (v.) **to give (me), please**

kudasaru (v.) **to give kindly (to me or my in-group) (polite)**

kūkō (n.) **airport**

kumoru (v.) **to get clouded**

kuni (n.) **country**

kurai (adj.) **dark**

kurasu (n.) **class**

kureru (v.) **to give kindly (to me or my in-group)**

kuroi (adj.) **black**

kuru (v.) **to come**

kuruma (n.) **car**

kutsu (n.) **shoes**

kyō (adv.), (n.) **today**

kyōkasho (n.) **textbook**

kyonen (n.) **last year**

mā mā (adv.) **so-so**

mada (adv.) **(not) yet, still**

made (p.) **as far as, until**

made ni (p.) **by, no later than**

mado (n.) **window**

mae (adv.), (n.) **before**

maiasa (adv.), (n.) **every morning**

maiban (adv.), (n.) **every night**

mainichi (adv.), (n.) **every day**

manshon (n.) **condominium**

mata (adv.) **again**

matsu (v.) **to wait**

me (n.) **eye**

meron (n.) **melon**

mēru adoresu (n.) **e-mail address**

merumaga (n.) **e-mail newsletter, blog**

michi (n.) **road, street**

mijikai (adj.) **short**

minasama (n.) **everyone, you all (very polite)**

minasan (n.) **everyone, you all (polite)**

minna (adv.), (n.) **all, everyone, you all**

miru (v.) **to see, to watch**

miruku (n.) **milk**

mise (n.) **store**

mo (p.) **also, too**

mo (p.) **(not) either, neither . . . nor**

mo (p.) **even**

mō (adv.) **already, more**

mokuyōbi (n.) **Thursday**

momo (n.) **peach**

mono (n.) **thing**

morau (v.) **to receive**

motsu (v.) **to hold**

motto (adv.) **more, much more**

muzukashii (adj.) **difficult**

nabi (n.) **navigation, navigation system**

nagai (adj.) **long**

nagara (p.) **as, while**

nakanaka (adv.) **at all, completely, quite, rather**

nakusu (v.) **to lose**

namae (n.) **name**

nan (pron.) **what**

nandemo (pron.) **anything**

nani (pron.) **what**

nanika (pron.) **something**

nanimo, nannimo (pron.) **nothing**

nannin (pron.) **how many people**

naosu (v.) **to fix**

naru (v.) **to become**

natsu (n.) **summer**

naze (adv.) **why**

ne (p.) **Don't you think so?, Isn't it?**

nedan (n.) **price**

neko (n.) **cat**

nekutai (n.) **necktie**

nemui (adj.) **sleepy**

neru (v.) **to sleep**

neteshimau (v.) **to fall asleep**

netto (n.) **Internet**

ni tsuite (ph.) **about**

ni (p.) **on, to**

nichiyōbi (n.) **Sunday**

Nihon (n.) **Japan**

Nihongo (n.) **Japanese (language)**

Nihonjin (n.) **Japanese**

niku (n.) **meat**

nikuya (n.) **butcher, butcher shop**

no (p.) **posessive marker**

node (p.) **because, since**

nomu (v.) **to drink**

noni (p.) **although, in spite of**

noru (v.) **to get on**

nōto (n.) **notebook**

nuru (v.) **to paint**

nusumu (v.) **to steal**

o (p.) **object marker**

obasan (n.) **aunt (someone else's)**

obāsan (n.) **grandmother (someone else's)**

oboeru (v.) **to learn**

ocha (n.) **Japanese tea**

ōdāmēdo (adj.) **custom-made**

ofuro (n.) **bath (polite)**

ohashi (n.) **chopsticks (polite)**

ohayō gozaimasu (ph.) **Good morning (polite)**

ohayō (excl.) **Good morning**

oikakeru (v.) **to chase**
oishii (adj.) **delicious**
ojiisan (n.) **grandfather (someone else's)**
ojisan (n.) **uncle (someone else's)**
okane (n.) **money (polite)**
okāsan (n.) **mother (someone else's)**
ōkii (adj.) **big**
omochi suru (v.) **to bring (polite)**
omoi (adj.) **heavy**
omoshiroi (adj.) **good, interesting**
omou (v.) **to think**
onamae (n.) **name (polite)**
oniku (n.) **meat (polite)**
onnanoko (n.) **girl, girls**
onnanokotachi (n.) **girls**
orenji (n.) **orange**
oriru (v.) **to get off**
osake (n.) **sake, rice wine (polite)**
ōsama (n.) **king**
oshieru (v.) **to teach**
osoi (adj.) **slow**
otegami (n.) **letter (polite)**
otearai (n.) **washroom, toilet**
otenki (n.) **weather (polite)**
otoko (n.) **male**
otokonoko (n.) **boy, boys**
otokonokotachi (n.) **boys**
otōsan (n.) **father (someone else's)**
otōto (n.) **younger brother**
ototoi (n.) **the day before yesterday**
owaru (v.) **to finish**
oyasai (n.) **vegetables (polite)**
oyogu (v.) **to swim**

pan (n.) **bread**
pasokon (n.) **personal computer**
purezento (n.) **gift**

raigetsu (n.) **next month**
raishū (n.) **next week**

reji (n.) **cashier**
rekishi (n.) **history**
rekōdo (n.) **record**
resutoran (n.) **restaurant**
ringo (n.) **apple**
rippa (adj.) **gorgeous**
rokugatsu (n.) **June**
rōmaji (n.) *romaji*, **roman letters**
ryokō (n.) **trip, travel**
ryōri (n.) **cooking**

saifu (n.) **wallet**
saikin (adv.) **recently**
sakana (n.) **fish**
sake (n.) *sake*, **rice wine**
samui (adj.) **cold (weather)**
san (n.) **Mr., Mrs., Miss, Ms.**
sangatsu (n.) **March**
sarani (conj.) **furthermore**
sashiageru (v.) **to give (to superiors)**
sashimi (n.) *sashimi*, **raw fish**
seiji (n.) **politics**
seijika (n.) **politician**
seiki (n.) **century**
seki (n.) **seat**
sensei (n.) **teacher, teachers**
senseitachi (n.) **teachers**
senshu (n.) **player**
senshū (n.) **last week**
sensō (n.) **war**
sētā (n.) **sweater**
shachō (n.) **company president**
shiawase (adj.), (n.) **happy, happiness**
shīdī (n.) **CD**
shigoto (n.) **work**
shika (p.) **just, only**
shiken (n.) **exam**
shimaru (v.) **to close**
shimau (v.) **to put away**
shinbun (n.) **newspaper**
shinpai suru (v.) **to worry**
shinsetsu (adj.) **kind**
shinsetsu ni (adv.) **kindly**

shinu (v.) **to die**
shiroi (adj.) **white**
shiru (v.) **to know**
shizuka (adj.) **quiet**
shizuka ni (adv.) **quiet, quietly**
shōjiki (adj.) **honest**
shōsetsu (n.) **novel**
shōsetsuka (n.) **novelist**
shū (n.) **week**
shūmatsu (n.) **weekend**
shuppatsu suru (v.) **to depart**
sō (adv.), (pron.) **in that manner, like that, that way**
sochira (adv.), (pron.) **there, that**
soko (adv.), (pron.) **there**
sonna (adj.) **that kind of**
sono (adj.) **that**
sonoue (conj.) **besides, furthermore**
sore (pron.) **it, that**
sorekara (conj.) **and then, and**
soretomo (conj.) **or**
soshite (conj.) **and, also**
subarashii (adj.) **wonderful**
sugi (adv.), (n.) **after, past**
sugu (adv.) **immediately**
suiyōbi (n.) **Wednesday**
suki (adj.) **to like**
sukiyaki (n.) *sukiyaki*
sukoshi (adv.) **a little, few**
sumu (v.) **to live**
sūpā (n.) **supermarket**
supōtsu (n.) **sports**
suru (v.) **to do**
sushi (n.) *sushi*
suwaru (v.) **to sit down**
suzushii (adj.) **cool**

tabemono (n.) **food**
taberu (v.) **to eat**
tabitabi (adv.) **often**
tabun (adv.) **maybe, perhaps, probably**
tachi (suffix) **plural marker**
taihen (adj.), (n.) **awful, bad**

taihen (adv.) **greatly, very (extreme degree, positive or negative)**
taisetsu (n.) **importance**
taitei (adv.) **generally, mainly, perhaps, probably**
takai (adj.) **expensive, high**
takusan (adv.) **a lot, many**
tamani (adv.) **occasionally**
tara (adv.) **if, when**
tatsu (v.) **to stand**
te (n.) **hand**
tēburu (n.) **table**
tegami (n.) **letter**
teinei (adj.) **polite**
tenisu (n.) **tennis**
tenki (n.) **weather**
terebi (n.) **TV**
to (p.) **together with**
to (p.) **if, when**
to (p.) **and**
tobu (v.) **to fly**
tōchaku suru (v.) **to arrive**
tokei (n.) **watch, clock**
tokidoki (adv.) **sometimes**
tokoro (n.) **place**
tomaru (v.) **to stay (overnight)**
toru (v.) **to take**
toshokan (n.) **library**
totemo (adv.) **very**
tsugi (n.) **next**
tsukareru (v.) **to get tired**
tsuki (n.) **month**
tsuku (v.) **to arrive**
tsukuru (v.) **to make**
tsumaranai (adj.) **boring**

uchi (n.) **home, house**
ue (n.) **top**
uma (n.) **horse**
umi (n.) **beach, sea**
untenshu (n.) **driver**
ureshii (adj.) **glad**

wa (p.) **topic marker**

wa (p.) **(emphatic and softening effect)**
waishatsu (n.) **dress shirt**
wakai (adj.) **young**
wakaru (v.) **to understand**
warui (adj.) **bad**
waruku (adv.) **bad, badly**
watakushi (pron.) **I, me**
watakushitachi (pron.) **we, us**

ya (p.) **and**
yachin (n.) **rent**
yagate (adv.) **soon**
yakyū (n.) **baseball**
yama (n.) **mountain**
yasai (n.) **vegetables**
yasashii (adj.) **easy**
yaseru (v.) **to get thin**
yasui (adj.) **cheap**
yasumu (v.) **to rest**

yo (p.) **(emphatic)**
yobu (v.) **to call**
yoko (n.) **side**
yōkoso (excl.) **welcome**
yoku (adv.) **better, much, often, well**
yomu (v.) **to read**
yori (p.) **than**
yoru (n.) **night**
yotto (n.) **sailboat**
yūbin (n.) **mail**
yūbinkyoku (n.) **post office**
yūgata (n.) **evening**
yuki (n.) **snow**
yukkuri (adv.) **slowly**
yūmei (adj.) **famous**

zenzen (adv.) **at all (with negative verbs)**
zuibun (adv.) **quite, rather**

Index

References in this index to the Basics, the Parts of Speech, and Special Topics are indicated by the symbol § followed by the decimal number.